Representing the Troubles: texts and images, 1970–2000

Representing the Troubles

Texts and Images, 1970–2000

Brian Cliff and Éibhear Walshe

EDITORS

FOUR COURTS PRESS

Published by
FOUR COURTS PRESS LTD
7 Malpas Street, Dublin 8, Ireland
email: info@four-courts-press.ie
http://www.four-courts-press.ie
and in North America by
FOUR COURTS PRESS
c/o ISBS, 920 N.E. 58th Avenue, Suite 300, Portland, OR 97213.

ISBN 1-85182-854-0

A catalogue record for this title
is available from the British Library.

Special Acknowledgment

This publication was grant aided by the

ROYAL IRISH ACADEMY

Printed in England
by MPG Books, Bodmin, Cornwall.

Contents

Acknowledgments

The editors wish to thank the staff at the Royal Irish Academy, and particularly Ruth Hegarty, for their invaluable support before, during, and after the conference. We also acknowledge our debt to the members of the Royal Irish Academy Committee for Anglo-Irish Literature, particularly Nicholas Grene and Terence Brown, Eilís ní Dhuibhne, Peter Denman, and Anne Fogarty. Finally, we are grateful to the contributors for their patiently helpful work. Éibhear Walshe would also like to thank Ciaran Wallace, and Brian Cliff would like to thank Molly Stevens and Michael Darcy for their help and support.

Introduction

This book has developed out of an April 2003 Dublin conference held under the auspices of the Royal Irish Academy Committee for Anglo-Irish Literature on the theme of 'Representing the Troubles'. During the two-day conference, academics and writers debated the ways in which fiction, drama, poetry, film, criticism and the visual arts have engaged with the past thirty years of political conflict in Northern Ireland.

On the first evening of the conference, Glenn Patterson, Anne Devlin, and Colm Tóibín discussed the relationship between art and politics in the North and the consequent implications for contemporary writers. Speaking first, the Belfast novelist Glenn Patterson talked about his sense that fictive meditations on political conflict can have the liberating potential for rewriting landscape and for re-appropriating language. As a way of contradicting monolithic political ideologies, he proposed the idea that literature can suggest a multiplicity of responses to questions of identity and to problems of political deadlock, thereby offering more than one possibility. The dramatist and short story writer Anne Devlin then drew on her experiences growing up in Belfast and her work as a teacher in a Protestant school to chart her own imaginative education, her coming to knowledge as a writer about Northern Ireland. She suggested that, for her, writing provided an imaginative arena where stories yet untold could finally be heard, where the missing elements within a culture and a society could be finally considered, and argued very strongly for the function of literature as an antidote to violence. Finally, the novelist Colm Tóibín, talking about his travel book *Walking Along the Border*, drew explicit links between contemporary and often contradictory accounts of sectarian murders in Northern Ireland and half-remembered tales of the Irish War of Independence overheard during his childhood in County Wexford in the 1960s. Tóibín's clearest sense was that a novelist is permitted to describe anything she or he wishes, and that this permission can open up our engagements with the nature of political violence in Northern Ireland and its ongoing cultural legacy.

The diverse essays that make up most of this collection interrogate the discourses surrounding political violence and reconsider the ways in which the political and the personal clash in the imaginative arenas of fiction and film, drama and the visual. Each of these critical voices is direct, independent, and questioning in its approach to the relations between art and politics in the context of the Troubles. Throughout, rather than coercing consensus, it has been our intention as editors to allow divergent and sometimes contradictory critical perspectives to sit side by side, as demonstrated, for example, by the distance between Des O'Rawe's and J'aime Morrison's views of the film *Some Mother's Son*. Still, a full generation after the onset of the latest Troubles, patterns of representation and analysis have begun to take a substantial, familiar shape, allowing us a vital and solid area for critical inquiry.

This coherence is, of course, particularly the case with literature of the Troubles, but, as O'Rawe and Gerardine Meaney argue, it is also the case with films, whether made in Ireland or America, and with critical responses, which (even from unconventional or skeptical perspectives) have begun to fall into familiar positions. While essays like those by Meaney, O'Rawe, and Richard Haslam question how critical and artistic responses become clichés, others – like those by Derek Hand, Jozefina Komporály, Jayne Steel, and Celia Keenan – focus instead on the struggles of writers and other artists to recognize and elude such clichés. Rather than confining themselves to tracing the contours of these positions, the contributors here also extend some familiar questions to areas that are under-considered in the emphatically literary Irish Studies field, areas like children's fiction, dance, and murals, where they usefully apply critical methods from more conventionally literary fields. In doing so, the contributors begin to revise these methods, and begin to define new and challenging questions for some of the more widely examined areas of Irish Studies.

Toward this end, many of the essays here examine relatively less-considered authors and emphasize narrative forms rather than the poetic forms that have often held most of the critical attention paid to representations of the Troubles and of Northern Ireland. A number of contributors (Haslam, O'Rawe, Keenan) seek to synthesize the materials in their genres, while others (Hand, Steel, and Komporály) take advantage of the past thirty years of studies to delve into material from new directions or to delve into new areas altogether (Morrison, Rolston, and Meaney).

In his essay on Benedict Kiely's 1985 novel, *Nothing Happens in Carmincross*, Derek Hand draws on a range of these approaches as he pinpoints the uncertainty and the deep-seated uneasiness about the nature of political violence within this narrative. Overall, Hand argues persuasively, there is a hesitation, even an unraveling, in this narrative of Northern Ireland. He posits the notion that this unraveling arises from a reluctance to connect imaginatively with the conflict, despite Kiely's own belief that this was his most serious and intense 'Troubles novel'. Hand identifies an unresolved tension between the representations of art and of history within Kiely's writing, and considers that the novel unconsciously demonstrates a kind of imaginative powerlessness when faced with the deadlock of political violence. This powerlessness is, as Hand suggests, of little use when attempting to imagine political realities and futures that could transcend violence.

Much as Hand does with *Nothing Happens in Carmincross*, Richard Haslam focuses on Bernard MacLaverty's *Cal* as a single novel that, with its explicit focus on the Troubles, is forceful enough to throw into sharp relief the blind spots of prevailing critical narratives. By 'subsuming *Cal* within generalizing accounts of the purported characteristics of contemporary fiction about Northern Ireland', he argues compellingly, the novel's sharpest critics effectively distort the novel 'for the cause of a critical meta-narrative about the artistic inadequacy and/or ideological delinquency of much Troubles fiction'. Haslam concludes that, by accurately depicting 'the politics of communal proximity' and critiquing 'the impoverished, theopolitical discourses of contemporary religious and political affiliation in the North of Ireland', *Cal* refutes the assertions of such critics that it fails 'to examine the complexity and ambiguity of social conflict'. This examination of the novel and its critics supports Haslam's return to the broader patterns of interpreting the literature of Northern Ireland, as he cautions against 'the seductive reductionism of a zero-sum exegesis'.

While Haslam presents *Cal* as a case study in the hardening of critical assumptions, Steel examines how a different but related set of assumptions are frustrated and evaded by women's fictions. Reading Deirdre Madden, Jennifer Johnston, Linda Anderson, and Mary Beckett, Steel draws on critical tools derived from French feminism and cultural materialism. She suggests that women's writing on Northern Ireland can disrupt a view of the history of women as a history of victimization, mainly by politicizing the private and the domestic. She reads Madden, Johnston, Anderson, and Beckett in an explicitly feminist context, seeing their writings as a challenge to patriarchal ideals about the nation and as a form of literary discourse that presents substantial alternatives to literary realism and to male-authored history. Finally, Steel suggests that a different kind of story, a missing part of the cultural history, is being re-appropriated in this politicizing of the private.

Bringing some of the same questions asked by Steel to bear on contemporary drama, Jozefina Komporály argues that, while 'family and motherhood have constituted a major concern in Irish drama', diverse alternatives have been overlooked, alternatives that have 'a looser connection to the personified nation'. By tracing these alternatives through the plays of Christina Reid, Anne Devlin, and Marina Carr, Komporály questions the equation of national identity with geography and shows how the 'political theatre' of these playwrights can 'reinterpret the very nature of the conflict'. Even Carr's 'seemingly non-political play' *Portia Coughlan* 're-politicizes the domestic by challenging age-old gender stereotypes' and 'vehemently disrupts the pattern of committed mothers in Irish drama, a pattern with which both Reid and Devlin engage'. Through such characters and such acts, Komporály concludes, these dramatists portray the family as 'symptomatic of the political struggle at large' and as containing 'the energies for psychological, social, and sexual regeneration'.

Where Komporály extends her analysis of the Troubles' context to the Republic by way of Marina Carr's Midlands, Gerardine Meaney analyzes the use of the Troubles as a backdrop in recent American films. Meaney discusses two mainstream Hollywood action thriller movies of the 1990s, *Patriot Games* and *The Devil's Own*, and locates these filmic representations of IRA activism within the context of American cultural discourses on terrorism, particularly in the aftermath of the Cold War. She explores the notion that the figure of the Irish terrorist in each of these films is deployed to counter anxieties about violent anti-government actions within the US, suggesting that the IRA man keeps the new threat at a comfortable distance by looking safely familiar but revealing himself as bigoted, driven, and murderous. She further analyzes the alienation of Northern Ireland in these mainstream American movies, which construct it as a place where memory, familial attachment, and loyalty have somehow become monstrous and inhuman. Meaney concludes convincingly that Northern Ireland operates as an oppositional place within American cinematic discourse, a place where the American audience is invited to contemplate images of itself that become reassuring when set against the ominously familiar-yet-foreign figure of the IRA terrorist.

In his essay, 'The Northern Other', Desmond O'Rawe continues this exploration of cinematic representations of political conflict in Northern Ireland, and posits the view that Irish cinema has failed to produce a genuinely political response. Building on his analysis of *December Bride* and *Michael Collins*, he asserts that a genuinely political cinema can only emerge in places where a vibrant and intellectually challenging film culture can exist. Drawing comparisons with other moments of political engagement in Russian, German, and Spanish filmmaking, O'Rawe believes that Irish cinema has been unwilling to subvert the representational regimes of its mainstream counterparts. He calls for Irish film criticism to challenge prevailing critical orthodoxies, and offers the suggestion that Irish cinema and Irish film criticism could profitably learn from comparisons with non-mainstream European and world cinema.

O'Rawe acerbically examines the deficiencies and limitations of Southern Irish films about the Troubles, and Meaney wittily critiques the clichés and contradictions of American films about the Troubles, but J'aime Morrison emphasizes what she sees as the more optimistic possibilities presented by dance, which, she argues, 'offers a way of conceptualizing movement as script for action'. Using the film *Some Mother's Son* and the short film *Dance Lexie Dance* to frame her analysis of images of dance in artistic and journalistic responses to the Troubles, Morrison asks how 'the body serves as a record of' the Troubles, 'as an embodied transcript'. After examining dance as 'a metaphor for action', Morrison goes on to analyse its invocation 'in the negotiations surrounding the Good Friday/Belfast Agreement as a metaphor for political progress' and its effect on those negotiations. Drawing on the 'social kinesthetic' she finds in a crowd's performance of the wave at a rally in Belfast, Morrison concludes that dance 'embodies the tensions and possibilities within the broader social and political configurations of Northern Ireland'.

While Morrison turns to dance, Meaney and O'Rawe to film, and Keenan to children's literature, Liam Kelly argues that visual artists in this generation have moved away from a lyrical pastoralism towards a more intellectual and discursive art. He supports this argument by examining the works of Northern artists like Willie Doherty, Rita Donagh, Paul Seawright and others. Similarly, Bill Rolston examines recent shifts in patterns of representation in the murals of Northern Ireland. Taking as his starting point arguments about attempts 'by people in groups to make sense of their world', Rolston looks at how the murals are used by different communities in Northern Ireland to 'articulate their political hopes and fears, their view of their own identity, their hopes of their past and future, and the political obstacles which they see'. Rather than simply providing visual propaganda, however, Rolston argues, 'each side's murals are about political mobilization within their respective communities'. To support this assertion, Rolston analyses the challenges faced by republican and particularly loyalist muralists in their respective approaches to the 'process of political imagination'. Loyalist muralists, he observes, may have struggled 'with constructing a myth of origin', despite their 'ingenious attempt … to reconstruct Cuchulain as a loyalist', but are clearly beginning to seek a colloquial brand of historical and political education within their communities.

Much as Rolston sees these murals as partial attempts by a given group (whether republican or loyalist) to educate itself about itself, Celia Keenan examines the shifting balance between the stereotypical and ecumenical elements of fiction written for children about the Troubles. Keenan examines the range of writings within the genre of children's fiction and suggests that much of this writing collapses into simplistic or reductive representations of cultural identity when dealing directly with fictional accounts of contemporary life in Northern Ireland. Often in these texts, as Hand has already noted about Benedict Kiely's novel, the writer's desire to appear 'impartial' and 'balanced' can diminish the narrative drive to confront notions of sectarian conflict. Interestingly, as Keenan remarks, when narratives written for children depart from a strictly realist format and instead deploy a kind of metaphorical obliqueness or use the genre of historical fiction, a more productive imaginative engagement with the realities of political conflict can result.

Keenan's essay provides a fitting note on which to close by reminding us of the limits on realism's ability to convey reality, and by returning to the sense of potential and future engagement with which this conference and this collection both began. We believe that, as they move between scepticism and optimism, between murals and movies, these lectures and essays explore a variety of challenging new perspectives on representations of Northern Ireland, and we hope that this volume will consequently provoke further original, stimulating debate on the role of art in a time of political conflict.

Brian Cliff and Éibhear Walshe
December 2003

Writing the Troubles

TALKS BY GLENN PATTERSON, ANNE DEVLIN AND COLM TÓIBÍN

Glenn Patterson

I recognize a few faces in the audience and they will know that I am going to take an unusual approach to this subject by talking largely about myself. After most readings there's usually a question and answer session, and questions that writers know to expect ... of course, '*Where do you get your ideas?*' For Northern Irish writers, the question that is most often asked is '*Do you think you would have written without the Troubles?*', which I answer with a straight face 'Yes', and then sometimes 'No'. I know what I can say with some certainty is that without the Troubles I wouldn't have travelled as widely across the world being asked the question. I am sure that most of you know that Irish writers don't emigrate any more, they just tour.

I suppose the question that really people are asking is to what extent has the Troubles influenced us, me, as a writer. As someone who was born in 1961, whose tenth birthday fell on 9 August 1971, the day when internment was introduced, whose twentieth birthday coincided with the death of a hunger striker, I think I would say fairly profoundly. Colm and I were on the radio yesterday, and Colm was talking about his *Walking the Border* book and being inspired to take that walk after the Anglo-Irish Agreement. In fact, though I had been writing fiction before that date, before November 1985, that moment did actually affect me in an immediate way. I was living in England in a house full of students, all of them English and I was watching the crowd of people who gathered outside the City Hall in Belfast to protest against the signing of the Anglo-Irish Agreement. Estimates of the numbers varied from 100,000 to 300,000, I think, a huge crowd. I was fairly certain that quite a number of people I had grown up with were there. I was a supporter of the Anglo-Irish Agreement and yet I had some sympathy with the people who were gathered outside City Hall, at least until they sacked Sammy Moore's sports shop, which is what they generally would do on these kinds of demonstrations. The people I was sharing a house with, on the other hand, were completely appalled by this demonstration of Britishness with which they felt no affinity whatsoever. There was a gap. The simplest reason I can think of why anyone would sit down and spend a year and a half, two years to write something that they hope will eventually be published as a novel is that there is a gap, there is something to write. Between this image of Northern Irish Protestants en masse outside the City Hall and the people I had grown up with in the sixties, there was a clear gap. Into that gap I wrote *Burning Your Own*, which was set in the summer of 1969.

The title came very late – the working title was *Dog Bag*, but that didn't seem to grab any of you! Very late on, I dipped into the manuscript, actually on the way to the publishing house, and I found a page where somebody talks about burning: 'we're a fierce lot for burning things, it's about time we started burning our own'. The implication was that we should turn some of the righteous anger that we usually direct outwards inwards, to look at ourselves a little bit more critically and put ourselves into our sustaining myths. I wrote that novel while I was living in England. I moved back to Belfast shortly after it was published because I had been trying to write another novel set in the then-present-day Belfast, the late 1980s, and found that every time I went back the present day Belfast I was writing about was then yesterday's Belfast. It kept changing. The bombers helped of course – they would remove good locations that looked like good places for your characters to live or work – but the redevelopers also helped by finally getting around to putting some new buildings into the city. This became part of the fabric of the novel, *Fat Lad*. It became a very important part of it – this novel was heavily influenced by a work of non-fiction, a Blackstaff Press book by Jonathan Bardon, *Belfast: An Illustrated History*.

Around this time I got to know Ciaran Carson, who was just about to publish *Belfast Confetti*, a work that had also been heavily influenced by Jonathan Barden's book. I think that what Ciaran's book did and what I hoped to do with *Fat Lad* was to look at the city of Belfast – a city that seemed to be a written story – as somewhere that was constantly in flux, as a city that was constantly being revised, a city where the actions of the citizens could revise the meaning of that city. *Fat Lad* grew out of that feeling that the city was constantly rewriting itself on the landscape. It also tried to look at what we now refer to as the totality of relationships. One of the things that had struck me in my reading of the fiction dealing with the Troubles was that very often we seemed to be looking at ourselves as characters in a story that could only be explained in terms of itself. I didn't know what it meant to be British or Irish, that we were meant to choose between one or the other, as was suggested to me when growing up. I didn't know what Irishness meant, I didn't know what it meant to be British, and so I wanted to bring into this novel some of the relationships between Northern Ireland and the rest of Ireland, between Northern Ireland and the rest of Britain and further afield, so there's an image which runs through the novel of the plane, the trails that planes left like threads in the sky tying us together.

This inquiry which I began in my second novel *Fat Lad* I continued in my third novel, *Black Night at Big Thunder Mountain*, where the totality of relationships was extended to include Germany in the 1960s, the USA in the 1960s, Yugoslavia during the time of the fall of Vukovar, and EuroDisney. I wanted to bring together as many experiences as possible, because it increasingly seemed to me that we needed to bombard our narrative with as many other narratives and story lines as possible. So I brought together a number of characters in *Thunder Mountain* in the heart of EuroDisney in 1991 and made them tell stories to each other for a night. I had for many years felt that that all the useful words have been taken away from us; you only have to watch the coverage of the most recent Gulf War to realize the crimes committed against language in any conflict. For many years, lots of the words that are the most beautiful and enabling of our language were being used by people who really meant the opposite of what they said when they talked about freedom and about justice.

There is a passage in *Black Night at Big Thunder Mountain* in which one of the characters talks to a man who made car bombs. It was a passage that came all at once, which is very rare for me, three or four pages all in one burst. I suppose what I wanted to know was this: if we could allow the words 'car bomb', if we could allow those words into our language, then what was to stop the words 'coffee-jar bomb', 'Cadbury's roses tin bomb'? Both of these we got. If you allowed those words not to go challenged, what was ultimately to stop human bomb? The answer is absolutely nothing, because that's what we ended up with, human bombs in Belfast, in Derry. Around the time that this novel was being written in the early '90s, I had moved back to Belfast from England, where I had been living. I was attracted back partly because I believed that there were people there who were trying to find ways of changing the vocabulary. I'm glad to say very many of them are people who are in the audience tonight.

Once the peace process began, shortly between me finishing *Thunder Mountain* and it coming out, we got our ceasefires. At this stage, I started getting phone calls from journalists in England, asking me the third big question: what on earth are you going to write about now that the story has been taken away from you? My answer to that is: I don't know, what have you been writing about in London, and how does an Aga work? What I did actually end up writing was *The International*, set a couple of years before even *Burning Your Own*, in 1967, on the eve of the first Civil Rights Association meeting. It was a story that came to me … in a way I was looking forward and looking back.

One of the things that developed after our cease fires, and it carried on into the political discussions that gave rise to the Belfast agreement, was the idea that we had to draw a line under the past. Unfortunately, very often we were talking about two different versions of the past, which were competing and very often violently. So I started to write *The International* shortly after I read of a speech given by Eddie McInteer, leader of the Nationalist Party, in Limerick on the weekend that I was interested in, when he talked of a change coming into Northern Ireland, perceptible only as 'a faint feeling of lightness in the air'. Knowing that a leader of the Nationalist party spoke in January 1967 about 'a faint feeling of lightness in the air' made me think that perhaps there were ways of reading that particular time forward from the moment rather than looking back on it.

The other thing that influenced that novel was that in the late 1990s, after the ceasefires, even after the Good Friday Agreement was signed, people were being murdered in Belfast. In 1967 a barman from the International called Peter Ward was murdered by the UVF, an appalling act that should have brought our country to a halt, but it didn't. In the 1990s they didn't kill people because of their religion, but they would call their victims drug dealers, and they would be killed in exactly the same way. I started to write *The International* in part to capture that 'faint feeling of lightness in the air', but also to try and go back to the first killings, as a reminder that we shouldn't just allow our citizens to be murdered and accept the terms of the people who killed them.

I suppose, in summing up, the novels that I have written to date have all been part of an enterprise to ask questions in another way. I don't think I know of a single novel that sets out to offer a solution to anything. No novel that I know, no good novel that I know, works as a political tract, because novels are too complex, they depend on conflict and on contradiction. But novels can ask questions and I started out to write novels to ask questions for myself. The big versions, the two big blocks in Northern Ireland, scream at you that things are like this and that it's whoever can win in whose version, that that's how they are. I think that what the novel can do, what poetry can do, what all art can do, is to add a qualification to the statement that things are like this. What art says is yes, it's like this, but also like this and like this and like this and like this.

Anne Devlin

The hard work of earning my living started when I went to teach in a school, Bushmills Comprehensive. I was interviewed for the job as the English and Drama teacher in May 1974 during the Ulster workers' strike. It was a Protestant school, in the heartlands of Paisley's constituency of North Antrim. The children lived behind the clock, it was a housing estate behind the town clock. They were out of time. I didn't manage to teach them Sean O'Casey. It was and still is my great failure. They regarded him as a republican propagandist and, knowing that I was a Catholic teacher, they wouldn't even allow me to take the book out of the cupboard. Then when Paisley came top of the polls in 1975 with the largest majority in the country, they celebrated with a rousing demonstration of Orange music in every single class-room during that day, except mine. I had the calmest day that I ever had at that school. And they taught me a great deal. Years later I wrote *The Venus De Milo Instead* about this school and about the fact that they actually introduced me to the idea of laughter to get over a difficulty. It's one of my most important discoveries, that my learning about my work and my whole commitment to what I think I'm doing as a writer goes back to those days in Bushmills.

If Coleraine University was the place where I rested up with literature when I was a student, it was in Freiburg University in the winter of '76 after leaving Bushmills that I began to write fiction. Incidentally, I felt that television in the '80s, which is when I was mostly writing, became very important after what I regarded as the vicious murdering decade which preceded it. The '80s was actually a very democra-tic time for the arts in Northern Ireland. We saw into each others' living rooms for the first time and we shared the same cultural events because the television drama didn't exist in that way beforehand and in some way has ceased to exist. I don't believe it would have been possible to arrive at the peace solution without the contribution of the television dramatists of the '80s, because I think that they were listened to. I believe that Graham Reid's *Billy* plays were listened to in the same way that my work-ing in Bushmills in the '70s allowed me to write *The Venus De Milo Instead* and gave me an introduction to a community that I felt had been locked away from me. That introduction was the real wall coming down for me. So, Coleraine University library was the place where I rested up with English because I basically went to university to get away from politics. I was a schoolgirl in the Civil Rights Movement – it was in Freiburg University in the winter of '76 that I first started writing fiction.

This writing was to do with being separated for the first time from the sounds of speech that made sense. I was freed in some way and it took me four years to get to have my first short story published, and it was a double blooming: I got my first radio play accepted as well. The radio producer was a very honest man, and it's very impor-tant to point out that such people existed. He told me that he couldn't talk to me until the government embargo on the subject was lifted. The play was *The Long*

March, about the hunger strikers. If he hadn't explained the embargo to me, I might have given up on my play because I might have thought that I had failed, where all that it meant was that I had to wait.

Most people start off with religion and lapse into politics – I started off with politics and lapsed into religion and it worked like this. I was a Marxist in my early affiliations and certainly culturally. The reason that I was a Marxist first and then became more spiritual goes back to a moment when I was on my way to mass at the age of four with my mother. My father doesn't go to mass, he reads the newspapers, and we passed by a gable end and above the painted lines of a goal post my mother points out our family name, my father's surname together with the letters VOTE NOW. Clonard Monastery I remembered as a baroque Catholic Church filled with the smoking gold urns and gold gates, flickering candles behind red stained glass and gladioli. I am looking at the prayer cards in my missal: a monk in a brown gown holding a boy in white by his shoulders, the boy holding up a bunch of white lilies, St Joseph's blessing; a small child on his own with a flock of lambs; a lady in a blue gown under cherry blossoms, with two white birds, holding an infant who in turn is holding out a perfect white disc to her little brother. I am pulled out of this pastoral reverie of doves and lambs and streams and flowers by my mother yanking my arm and drawing me out of the crush of bodies in the long pew, and I wonder what I have done. We are not alone in leaving the church. Someone is shouting and then I know it is not me, it is not my fault, it is something that is being said, which my mother told me when we got outside the church: 'They called your father the antichrist'. Now I had an Auntie Mary, so I didn't think there was anything wrong with that. But then I knew that there was something wrong because later my mother told me 'They said your daddy hit me and he drank'. So if you can understand that when you are alienated as a child and your family is alienated from your religious background, Marxism seems to be the solution up to a point.

'Where was I when poetry called to me', says Neruda. Contrary to what I had been led to believe, the Call is not to a religious vocation; the Call is the call to writing. The place the library, another library, the library at Leeds University with a copy of Jorge Luis Borges's 'Fictions' and the short story 'The South'. Bound tightly in the nutshell of this perfect story is the whole cameo of an approach to writing. Scheherazade. The role of the woman is to cure the man of his murderous impulses by telling him a number of stories. The stories hold him. As long as she keeps telling the stories, she will live. And of course by the end he is transformed. They might stay together, they might not, the point is that he is transformed by the wazir's daughter's voice. I was so impressed by this idea as an antidote to violence as I read it in Leeds

University all those years ago. I began to read *1001 Nights*. But Borges's short story 'The South' contains a warning against this kind of retreat. The protagonist is so busy reading the book that he bumps his head and he has an accident which leads him to going on a journey which will take him to his death. You cannot make decisions about life or make practical arrangements in the frame of mind that creates and inhabits the world of fiction. 'The South' is the past where he is known by his family name only and where his death awaits him.

I wrote two stage plays between 1985 and 1994: *Ourselves Alone*, from the bipolar axis of my student attachment to Marxism, and *After Easter*, from the diametrically opposed axis of spirituality. My unconscious simply banged like a drum on the doors of my perceptions and demanded to be included. And this fact alone, this invasion of consciousness in the decade of terror – which is what the '70s was – is largely responsible for my approach to writing.

The Troubles began in 1969 and death announced itself in my dreams. It was a coffin going around a house. A woman was leading the mourners and she was blindfolded. When it ends, I am in Paris, in a skyscraper, near the Champs de Mars. I look out at the sky mirrored in the opposite skyscraper, a grid of glass squares. It measures a piece of the sky and cloud. A piece of the sky had been mapped, a piece of eternity, of infinite space. Will you remember us, a son of a man who has died is saying on the tv. Writing has to change now that the Agreement is signed. Instead of writing what we remember, I'd like to write about what is missing. It's time to give up the death instinct. The trouble is – we're not in a good place to do this at the moment, but we have to make a start.

Stones

For nor reason I gathered stones
at Brandon Head after a swim
moss green, wine red, black and tan
and most of all grey
for no reason but to mark the day.
Within a week
my father took his glasses off for the last time
handed them to me
and closed his eyes.
I wondered why a man who couldn't see wore his glasses in bed.
He used the table to guide him through the room
my mother said. I only kept it there for him.

Two days after his funeral
she moved the table into the parlour bay.
For some reason I remember
a small photo my aunt sent in '64?
Of clouds spreading across table mountain-
at the awesome sight of the cloudscloth
he uttered disapproval:
Ay - but Mandela?
The grainy image of the stone table remains
as majestic as his prescence by my mother
writing replies to the condolences
on an embroidered cloth in the bay.
My aunts green and gold, the blue and purple stitched threads,
honouring a man who could oppose such things.

My last sight of him
framed by a window dashed with rain
overlooking the outside wall of the empty prison
above the drone and rumble of a JCB
crunching stones
his grizzled grey head above a cuff of sheet
in a cot bed,
turned on his side, asleep.

In the months following 9/11, I went with my family to South Africa because I wanted to go somewhere that I felt the hard work of maintaining peace was being done. As well as the usual attractions I went to Robbin Island on a pilgrimage. After Mandela's cell, we went to the lime quarry and found the cave that the prisoners used as protection from the sun. It was in this cave that the African National Congress gave birth to its university and drew up policies for the future of their country. Outside, in the middle of the quarry, stood a flock of blue-clad school children who were gathered with their teacher by a pile of stones. Each stone, she explained, had been placed by a returning prisoner to Robbin Island as a sign they had survived. So that's what the pile of stones was for. One of the circumstances of the past has been writing from within trauma. It will take a little while before the prisoners realise that the doors of the prison are open and when they do they will start to return and the name on the first stone will be awareness.

Colm Tóibín

The deaths came singly and the journalists by that time had run out of strategies to report each one as though they were the most important thing that had ever happened, and to believe that the items on the news and the news editors were operating to an agenda which was very close, embedded in the human agenda, which is that certain things are more interesting than others. The mind is a monkey and the mind moves on. I blundered into this in July of 1986 and in recording this event, it is important that this event doesn't stand for the other events. It is on its own that day, 8 July 1986, when the IRA killed murdered, shot, whatever word you want to use – and the words will depend on which side you were on at the time, which words you want to use – they shot John McVitty in a field in Fermanagh, close to the border with Co. Monaghan, and they went over the border. I came from outside, so far outside indeed that none could understand my pronunciation of the place where the funeral was to happen. I would have called it Achadrumsee but locally it seemed to just melt into aadrims. I couldn't say it. It seemed to be a different language, it was a different religion, I suppose, from my religion, which was Catholicism.

I went there, it was immensely sad. He was a UDR man, and he was on his tractor. Like a lot of UDR men, he was a part-time UDR man and he was a farmer. He was very vulnerable because his farm was close to the border, isolated and close to Lackey Bridge, which meant that his killers could easily escape. He was with his 7-year-old son, who has to be 25 now, and they shot him and they ran away. He was now in his coffin. It was one of those lonely Church of Irelands that are all over this island, and the bishop came and his local pastor. The family was grief-stricken; 'grief-stricken' isn't the word for how they held each other, or for their shock, even though this was right in the middle of those years when people like that were being picked off. Again, I use that word advisedly, picked off, murdered, shot, whatever, killed. There were others, colleagues of his and friends of his who were the same age as him, who lay in the graveyard with their gravestones marked 'murdered by the IRA'. And there were no television cameras there. This was 1986: a single killing of a UDR man in the south of Fermanagh would not have been worth that day's news, not with the resources that news editors have, with the interests that people who watch television have. It would not have been an item on the news. The killing itself would have been an item on the news, the murder itself, but not the actual funeral. I wished everyone could have seen the faces. Not only that, but the sermon, which went unrecorded in any of the papers. He simply listed the murdered dead in Fermanagh since the Troubles had begun. He just simply stood up and listed their names. One by one.

Some of their names I recognized and remembered, but most of their names I didn't recognize or remember. He just wanted to ask, 'Have we been abandoned? What has happened to cause this long list of names of the murdered dead and yet so few convictions for those who did the killings?' I was writing a book, I was a journalist. I went then to find out, to the other side of the border. I asked people, since these people who committed this crime had escaped across the border, 'Did the guards come out from the local garda station? Had they seen anything strange the day before or that day or had indeed they seen the murders?' No.

Everyone assured me that 'the guards never come out here'. So, it wasn't just that it was the funeral. That was another statistic, another unreported event. The crime itself remains not just undetected but not even investigated. And the attempt then to find a pattern. I went to talk to the pastor about these killings. I read as much as I could about the area. I discovered certain things which were useful and interesting. One suggested that the IRA were slowly picking off the only sons of Protestant farms in Fermanagh, which turned out not to be true. There were a lot, obviously, because of the nature of these farms, with only one son working on them, but of course there was often a brother working somewhere else. Or they were only children, but it wasn't a deliberate activity, it couldn't have been because the killers came from Tyrone or Monaghan. They didn't really know about the families, they weren't locals, they weren't exactly neighbours. So that attempt to find a pattern didn't really work.

There was a suggestion that this killing was done in a retaliation for the killing of an IRA man Seamus McElwain. People suggested that John McVitty might have been present at that killing. That, however, turned out to be possible, but not true. Then of course, the idea – slowly, because it came from outside – trying to work out who joined the UDR? Why did they join the UDR? I discovered that joining the UDR was a common and easy form of comradeship and friendship among young Protestant men in that area at that time. While they might have been seen by the other side – the side that at some stage in my life I have called my side – as harassing them, the harassment, when I went to find out what it was, was low-level harassment: being stopped in a car, being stopped a second time, being asked your name, being asked your name twice, being stopped later on.

What I then discovered was that, though we know so much about this place in Northern Ireland, there was no such place called Northern Ireland. There was no pattern which went down from Derry into Belfast and down into south Armagh and over into Fermanagh. That, in general, there was no picking off of Catholics in the streets of Fermanagh as there had been in Belfast. I suppose I want to use the word innocent there. In the reports, there was this sense of sectarian violence, of tit-for-tat violence, of Protestants who drove around at night trying to find Catholics, about which we've read so much and heard so much. Oddly enough, despite these killings, what happened in Fermanagh in those years was different from what happened in Belfast, different from what happened in Tyrone, and different from what happened in Derry. I was working at that time as a reporter, and while I had written a novel and was thinking about novels, not only did the idea in those days that I should somehow fictionalize this not occur to me, but, if it had occurred to me, I would have dismissed it immediately as the last thing that I needed to do just then. What I needed to do was to find out as much as I could about patterns that might explain this, to try to make connections and disconnections and, as it were, explanations. If there were none, point out there were none and publish this, write this as clearly as I could and publish it, get it into the public domain to be read by as many people as I possibly could.

What also occurred to me was that I was fascinated by the boy who is now 25, who is now, I suppose, being asked to vote for what we might call the peace process, or for candidates who support the peace process. I wonder what his view on David Trimble might be, just now as further agreement is being made, as the killers of his father have never even been sought or come forward, or no one has ever attempted to do truth and reconciliation, while the Saville inquiry goes on in London, which I personally fully support. One wonders whether, as he goes through and reads now about the second inquiry, he asks why there was never a first inquiry for John McVitty, who was killed, murdered, shot dead by the IRA on 8 July in 1986. What did occur to me, however, was what would it be like for his son in the future, when things have settled down, as things will in that area, when things will be told as stories, half-forgotten, half-remembered, seldom mentioned, sometimes mentioned? What would it be like for his son, if his son suddenly realized that he wanted to work with words, that there was something in him, that the dark spaces in him, or the spaces within could be used in that way?

And that in fact was who I am, who I was, who I am the grandson of, brought up in the area that Michael Ryan mentioned, with Vinegar Hill across the way. You could see it all the time and what happened in 1798 was constantly mentioned, but there had also been a 1916 rising of a sort in our town, Enniscorthy, when there had been a Black and Tan war, or War of Independence, depending again on which term you wanted to use. There had been a civil war in that area, and my uncle and my grandfather had been involved in that, as I heard. Imagine the grandchildren of the other side who would hear your grandfather, you know, sixty years ago, went over Lackey Bridge one day, just a story being told. 'I was doing a job on the other side', and you would say, 'What do you mean, a job?' You would half-know, half-hear the half-remembered, half-forgotten things about the past, about the violent past, about that past that is both haunting and always in the background. For me as a novelist it was the period afterwards that interested me, that concerned me as a novelist to dramatize. I believe that the novelist has a right to describe anything, from sex, any form of sexual activity, any level of detail, any level of violence, any war the novelist wishes to describe, that there are no forms and no rules about who can write what, and that you can write novels about anything. We have fought these battles to describe what we wish to describe for a long time, we're not giving up on them now. But from my own point of view, what concerned me personally at that time was that my mind worked towards describing what happened to John McVitty that day, while my imagination worked separately to try to describe what had happened to me as someone who came in my own life sixty, seventy years after those events had happened in my place, events which had been, as I say, half-remembered, half-forgotten.

Something happened: Benedict Kiely's *Nothing Happens in Carmincross* and the breakdown of the Irish novel

DEREK HAND

In the seventeen-year period between 1968 and 1985, two works by Benedict Kiely confronted directly the realities of the situation in the North of Ireland: an extended short story *Proxopera* (1977) and *Nothing Happens in Carmincross* (1985). Both were widely praised on publication for their depiction of the violence of the Troubles, with some critics also celebrating their analysis of this violence. What is noteworthy about these responses is how critics mostly fail to register the quite obvious uncertainties and uneasiness at the heart of both these works, and especially with regard to *Nothing Happens in Carmincross*. These uncertainties thoroughly undermine any such attempts at straightforward and simple interpretation. My interest is not so much in how *Nothing Happens in Carmincross* might be a successful confrontation and representation of the violence that beset modern Ireland for thirty years, but rather in how the novel flirts with failure on a number of crucial levels. This essay will explore those aspects and moments within the novel when the narrative undermines itself and breaks down, thus registering formally the crisis that the Troubles present for a culture attempting to move into a future where violence and conflict will no longer exist.

It has been argued that the Troubles' influence on Benedict Kiely's fiction was to make it 'more sombre, more intense, [and] less comic' (D. Casey, *Contemporary Irish Novelists,* 26). Certainly, for a writer known for the accessibility of his short stories that follow closely the form of the oft-told tale well told, *Proxopera* and *Nothing Happens in Carmincross* clearly offer the reader something much more consciously disturbing. The concentrated brevity of *Proxopera* confines this story concerning the use of proxy bombers by the IRA to a single note of seething anger at the atrocities tearing apart a community. Novelist Jennifer Johnston said of *Proxopera* that, despite the positive critical reception it received in England and Dublin, 'it was a hysterical scream, and it was not true. It was a load of romantic rubbish' (Myers, 23).

Such criticism, perhaps, misses the point that anger is certainly a legitimate response to the horrors of bloodshed. Nor does it concede that a retreat into a nostalgic past and a celebration of 'old decency' might be a necessary manoeuvre when the present appears so unbearable. However, it does hint at the deeper malaise of paralysis that occurs when such a response substitutes for any real engagement with the underlying issues causing violence. In other words, no answer or imaginative thought can be given to solving the problem and moving into the future when outrage is the only reaction permitted.

Proxopera allowed Kiely to document his indignation at a situation that was all but destroying the place and the people he had celebrated in early work such as *Land without Stars* (1946) and *In a Harbour Green* (1949). It seems clear that the author himself saw *Nothing Happens in Carmincross* as the more substantial and serious treatment of the Troubles. In an interview he said that he felt it was an unpleasant task to write it, and that he had wished he could have written a happier book, but that it was 'a novel he felt impelled to do' (Allen, 12).

Nothing Happens in Carmincross centres on Mervyn Kavanagh, an academic plying his trade in America, who is returning to Ireland to attend the wedding of his favourite niece in Carmincross, a small border town in Northern Ireland. His journey there from Shannon Airport is a picaresque affair, progressing jaggedly from episode to episode, with the loose plot only held together by the rambling consciousness of Kavanagh and by the ever-present Troubles, in the form of bombings and shootings relayed over the radio, television, and newspapers. Kavanagh's marriage in America is failing, his affair with his old flame Deborah fails, and of course, tragically, the purpose of his visit does not come to pass because his niece is blown to bits in the process of posting a few final wedding invitations.

James M. Cahalan suggests that *Nothing Happens in Carmincross* returns to the basic structure of the Irish novel, with the arrival of the 'interested outsider' to Ireland (265). If this is the case, from the beginning of the novel the suggestion is offered that what will be on show is the objectivity of the outsider. However, Kiely complicates this simple proposition by having his protagonist be *both* an outsider *and* an insider.

While this instance of confusion might seem somewhat insignificant, it does disturb the reader's engagement with the novel. Mingling two possible perspectives in this way means that the narrative fluctuates between the poles of hope and despair. In other words, having Kavanagh come to Ireland from abroad suggests that a new vision of Ireland's problems is possible and that the paralysis of 'anger' on show in *Proxopera* can be challenged and perhaps overcome. Being detached and apart will allow him the authority and control to envisage an 'end' or a solution, as it were. But, that he is, in fact, returning 'home' – even if it is only for a short visit – means that such a disinterested, aloof, perception might not be possible at all.

Clearly a concern with knowledge is fundamental to the novel. That Mervyn Kavanagh is an academic obviously elevates the status of knowledge and knowing within the text. Certainly the range of reference on display within the work is encyclopaedic: songs, ballads, poems, anecdotes, history, and literature are all part of the knowledge employed by Kavanagh. It is worth noting how coy contemporary reviewers of the novel were in relation to Kavanagh's academic discipline, none of them committing themselves to saying what it is exactly that he teaches. In the book itself though, it seems clear that he is an historian:

> – Would you read a book of mine if I gave it to you?
> – Read a history book? That's what you write, isn't it? Whatever for?
> I know my history. (Kiely, 56)

As does his position as an outsider, Mervyn Kavanagh's role as an historian leads the reader to expect the kind of distanced objectivity traditionally associated with that discipline. It would seem then that the intention is to focus on Ireland's Troubles from a position of impartiality, to consider the facts of Irish history in order to come to some understanding of contemporary violence.

In postmodern fashion, history itself as a subject and a discourse is interrogated. At one stage Kavanagh offers this assessment: 'Marx suggested that history repeats itself, second time as farce. Marx was too kind. History is farce the first time. God only knows what it is, second time round' (Kiely, 39). A question is raised whether 'history' can tell us anything about the present moment; in other words, what lessons can we take from the past that will bring comprehension in the present? Of course, the spectre of 'eternal recurrence' alluded to here is important, suggesting that there is nothing that can be gleaned from concentrating on the past. In a contemporary interview, Kiely says: 'History, so to speak, has let us down. We have let history down, nobody ever learns anything' (Allen, 12).

As if to emphasize this, the juxtaposition of past and present in the novel establishes the past as the more hospitable place. One critic declares that 'the presence of the past conveys always an acute sense of loss and of the inferiority of the present to the past' (D. O'Brien, 33). Kiely was himself blunt when questioned about this aspect of the novel: 'That's pretty obvious, you know, if you are living in a society in which people are murdering one another' (Myers, 85). Perhaps, as was the case with *Proxopera*, Kiely's past is a sentimental and nostalgic creation rather than a factual reality. Nonetheless, rendering the past as a site of edenic possibility in comparison to the horrors of the present forcefully registers for the reader the fault line between the two time zones.

And yet, Kiely does want to present continuities between past and present in the form of Republican violence and Republican ideology. On one of his many rambling excursions, Kavanagh visits the home of an elderly IRA man who says of the present violence in the North: 'If I wasn't so old I'd make the journey up there to see how the boys are doing in O'Neill's Tyrone' (Kiely, 73). Conor Cruise O'Brien, reviewing the novel in the *New York Review of Books*, also discerns order and unity in the text and a very clear relationship between the past and the present:

> What I found most haunting [about] *Nothing Happens in Carmincross* was the sense of the continuity and inner logic of the culture of Catholic Ireland: the ballads, the folk traditions, the received version of history, the popular assumptions, even the jokes, in a way pushing us unwittingly along in the direction of holy war. (42)

Conor Cruise O'Brien's arguments about the continuities in nationalist Irish culture are well known and, quite obviously, he applies that argument to this novel. His vision is of a seamless Irish culture, sleepwalking into the future, unaware of the potential for violence that it may encourage. The main problem with this argument is that it imposes a retrospective coherence on political and cultural movements that they did not, and do not, possess. Inherent within the argument is an implication that Irish nationalist culture has an assertive confidence, without any room for uncertainty or critique. As regards this particular novel, O'Brien's analysis is one more example of how, in an Irish context, aesthetic values can be overridden by political or ideological concerns.

Art, happily, always has more to offer than mere narrow ideology and politics can, and is open to numerous readings and interpretations. This is certainly the case with Benedict Kiely's *Nothing Happens in Carmincross*. Whatever the author's intention might have been and whatever certain commentators impose upon the text, the text reveals itself to be a much more hesitant and questioning narrative than one that makes definite or final conclusions or comments on the nature and violence of the Troubles. While an ordered narrative is what is striven for, in fact what is achieved is quite the opposite. Instead of unity and coherence what, in truth, the reader encounters is a text undergoing a process of ongoing unravelling, so that the form of the novel in its embodiment of dysfunction and breakdown mirrors the horrors it attempts to contain.

One of the central elements of the novel is, as has been noted, having the protagonist be an historian. On the surface it conveniently allows Kiely to range easily through Irish history, making connections and comparisons between the past and the present. Coupled with Kavanagh's numerous jaunts round the countryside, this offers the reader both a history and a tour of the country, signalling that Ireland's struggles operate in the realms of both land and narrative.

The purpose of this journey is to understand the bomb in Carmincross:

> To you there far away in America, and far away from me and everything that I belong to or that belongs to me, or that, for good or bad, made me what I am, it may be difficult to explain how or why destruction came to Carmincross. (Kiely, 256)

Kiely has said that in writing the novel he had to work back from the moment of the bomb blast in an effort to make the series of events and moments link toward the final, horrible consequence (Myers, 86). In other words, he wants to discover, through his character Mervyn Kavanagh, why something happened where, for so long, nothing much had ever happened.

One critic mentions the novel's 'extraordinary, almost maniacal, attention to detail' (Pelaschair, 78). However, it is not simply the detailed facts of history that are interesting to Mervyn Kavanagh, so too are songs, poems, and anecdotes. Indeed, not unlike John Banville's unnamed historian in *The Newton Letter: An Interlude*, Kavanagh appears to be a closet novelist and poet. His fascination is with the past as mediated through song and story more so than with the past as mediated through the hard facts of history. For him, it seems, these songs, ballads, and poems are of similar value to the specifics of Irish history in trying to come to some form of understanding regarding the violence of the present. Conor Cruise O'Brien's thesis is obviously born out of this juxtaposition of fact and fiction, of art/culture and history. Thus his famous phrase concerning the 'unhealthy intersection' would seem to explain this, for him, unholy alignment (quoted in Longley, 648). Yet, as in John Banville's novel, there exists a tension between fact and fiction, a debate as to fiction's value for understanding the present moment. As an historian Kavanagh is unsure whether his discipline possesses a more privileged access to truth than is possible though literature. He is drawn to the claims of both, but cannot choose between them: the result is that this tension between art and history remains troublingly unresolved at the close of the novel.

It is at the level of form that these uncertainties manifest themselves most clearly. That the narrative is told from Mervyn Kavanagh's point of view means that his own anxieties about his position as both an outsider and insider, as well as his concerns with the power of knowledge and the relationship between historical fact and historical fiction, become the readers' anxieties. In other words, his epistemological unease regarding the power of different 'narratives' reveals itself in his narrative, so that his own position as both author and authority is questioned.

The novel opens with a Prologue, or 'Reveille' as Kiely labels it, of four mostly well-known quotations from the past. We have 'History is a nightmare from which I am trying to awake' from James Joyce, 'We had fed the heart on fantasies / The heart's grown brutal from the fare' from W.B. Yeats, a quote from John Henry Newman referring to his vision of Ireland in a hundred years to come and then, almost inevitably, we have Eamon de Valera's 'comely maidens' speech. The first two are said to be 'Extravagant statements by two well-known Irishmen', the third 'A quite crazy statement by a well-known nineteenth-century Englishman', and the last 'An euphoric or idiotic statement by a well-known twentieth-century Irishman of Spanish and Irish origins' (Kiely, 9–10). There is a power play at work here. Kiely withholds the names of the authors of these words till the end of the novel when he includes them in his acknowledgements, thereby putting himself into an hierarchical position in relation to his supposedly less-informed readership. The significance of these quotations should be clear: the illusions and the delusions of the past, of Irish history, need to be challenged and overcome in the present violent moment. It is Kiely's display of jocular and nonchalant authority that these 'comments' attest to that the reader should note closely.

A similar authoritative posture is taken up by the character Mervyn Kavanagh, whose knowledge, as we know, ranges over Irish and world history and, of course, literature, plucking quotations, stories, and facts from the past in his effort to impose meaning upon the present. He is, as he himself declares, 'good at such things (after all they gave him money for it in the USA)', and can therefore 'provide the relevant text' (Kiely, 77). Kavanagh, like Kiely, hopes to be confidently in command of his material and can, hopefully, impose some shape and order on the narrative he relates. However, the author's intention might not always be clear, as one critic points out:

> His tone is frequently elusive: irony and sarcasm as he uses them can be easily mistaken for comedy, flippancy, simple digression. (Flower, 314)

Again, the difficulty for the reader is in discerning the aspirations of the author/narrator: are we meant to be entertained by this response to violence and upheaval or should we be troubled by it? And, of course, the mischievously playful tone on show at the outset – and continued throughout – is savagely undermined in the novel itself, where the humour and comedy is bleak and black rather than light and entertaining.

Kavanagh, as both outsider and insider, is caught between an act of condemnation and celebration. He desires on the one hand to denounce those elements in Irish history and culture that might be the basis of the present Troubles. On the other hand, he seems overly eager to keep his readership amused with his vociferous rejoicing in all things Irish. At one point he bemoans the fact that 'The old songs have been polluted' (Kiely, 47), which might be said to defend them from the charge of giving succour to the men of violence in the present day. In consequence, his narrative struggles to find an appropriate tone by which the reality of Ireland can be approached. The use of songs and stories might be a means of acknowledging this position, as if Kavanagh wants to conceal – or dispel – the brutal facts of Irish history behind the warm glow of seemingly benign culture and art. And yet this is not possible, as his narrative is constantly interrupted by the need to relate more facts of violence and destruction.

While this might appear, at one level, to be a rigorous consideration of the relationship between art and history in Irish culture, demonstrating the links and the tensions in that relationship, it is, in fact, far from being so. An early reviewer of the novel claimed that it 'is discursive to the point of being chaotic' and that overall it suffers from a 'woeful lack of coherence' (Dunne, 225). In other words, the implied 'control' and 'authority' that is needed for a coherent argument to emerge from within the narrative is thoroughly absent. Kavanagh is unable to move toward any end in his geographical and intellectual meanderings: each new locale throws up another anecdote or poem or ballad which in turn leads on to more poems, references, and stories. Everything appears to be already said: the future is the past because there is no escape from this relentless intertextuality. Nothing is allowed to be what it is as everything is 'like' something else. In a way he is very much like the Collector as delineated by Walter Benjamin, who says of the action of collecting in the modern world:

> What is decisive in collecting is that the object is detached from all its original functions in order to enter into the closest conceivable relation to things of the same kind. This relation is the diametric opposite of any utility ... (204)

With so many references, the usefulness of the 'past' is contested. Any final meaning or significance is denied as no order can be applied. Most contemporary reviewers of the work fail to acknowledge this obvious feature of the work, a feature that undermines any claims it may have to being a well-structured response to the violence of the 1970s and 1980s. Most are happy to impose – as Conor Cruise O'Brien does – order and stability where there is none.

It must be said that one of the very strong qualities of Benedict Kiely's novels before *Nothing Happens in Carmincross* is his employment of straightforward narrative techniques. His novels of the 1940s and 1950s do not manifest the kind of difficulties with classic realism that so much Irish fiction does. His novels are remarkably unself-conscious with regard to form: their coherency and clarity reflect the author's vision of what he perceives to be the stable society out of which he writes. This is not to claim that Kiely is unaware of form, for in a later novel such as *The Cards of the Gambler* (1953), he is able to combine a traditional Irish folktale with his contemporary story of a Faust-like relationship with the devil. Also, in *Dogs Enjoy the Morning* (1968), his last novel before *Nothing Happens in Carmincross*, Kiely energetically blends poetry, prose, myth, and legend in this mad tale of Irish midland life. It is a novel bubbling over with joyous vitality, with Kiely's overt acknowledgement of both oral and literary influences indicating that the emphasis at this juncture is very much on a celebration of Irish culture and Irish narratives. His mingling of different genres signals that Ireland is a site of the fantastic: a place of possible freedom and escape where reality can be imaginatively transformed.

Kiely employs a similar narrative technique in *Nothing Happens in Carmincross*, but in this novel, dealing as it does more with death than life, it cannot be used to delight in the textures of Irish culture. As one critic puts it, what the reader is presented with in *Nothing Happens in Carmincross* is 'a kind of stream-of-nightmare lament for the blood strewn province', with the lament finally giving way to depression (D. Casey, *Contemporary Irish Novelists*, 26). That difference, in itself, registers the altered situation brought about by the outbreak of violent upheaval in Northern Ireland. Laura Pelaschair claims that *Nothing Happens in Carmincross* is 'densely written and stylistically complex', an intertextual tangle that is 'purposefully disorientated' (78). If this is so, then why is this disorientating narrative presented to us?

My brief outline of the plot touched upon some of Mervyn Kavanagh's failures in terms of his personal life. There is also his failure as an historian to come to grips with an Irish past and his problems in differentiating clearly between fact and fiction. Linked to this is his inability to discover an appropriate tone in which to approach and relate his material. Of course, the bomb itself is a signal of failure – as is all war in the modern world – but so is, ultimately, the lack of understanding about what really led to this bomb being set off and the lack of imagination as to what steps might be taken to ensure that no more bombs will explode in Carmincross or, indeed, anywhere else. By the close of the novel, Kavanagh is no closer to understanding why this occurred, despite his best efforts and despite his knowledge of Ireland's history.

Kevin Casey, in reviewing the novel for the *Irish Times*, says that it 'mourns the present *senseless* eruption of violence' and that the bomb emphasises '*senselessness* and waste'. Ultimately, Casey claims that by the close of the novel what we see is that 'Life goes on. Another *meaningless* act is about to become another memory' (10; emphasis mine). It is the overuse of the terms 'senseless' and 'meaningless' here that is of interest. Of course, this language and thinking is outside Kiely's text but it is echoed within the novel itself, which reflects and generates its own kind of meaninglessness and senselessness.

It is an odd experience on first reading this novel from the vantage point of the present. It struck me that Time within the novel is very fluid, with references to the 1970s and 1980s – the period in which the novel was written – occupying the same 'time' of the novel. There is, basically, no chronological structure to the narrative. Kiely, in his 'Last Post' at the end of the novel, suggests that this chronological disorder does not really matter:

> The earnest students of atrocities will detect anachronisms. Specimens have been moved about in time. And in place. Does it matter? (267)

It is a curious admission on his part, especially in a work in which such efforts are made to hold Irish history and myth to account for present-day ills. One result of his almost casual indifference is that a crucial gauge of meaning, that is time/progression, is utterly undone within the text. It was a novel about fourteen years in the writing, and it is as if each year, each new outrage and atrocity had to be incorporated. It is as if Time itself has been bombed into submission. The nightmare within the novel is that everything – all actions, all knowledge – is collapsed in an ever-present moment of meaninglessness. In this world there can be no transcendence, no knowledge, no understanding or revelation because, finally, nothing means anything, given that nothing is allowed to mean anything by the novelist.

It could be suggested that myth is that which underlines unity within the text. Kavanagh and his lover Deborah are likened to Diarmuid and Gráinne as they flee the jealous pursuit of Deborah's husband Timothy. Yet, this too is undermined because Kavanagh is also Merlin the wizard and Mandrake the Magician. High and low culture is made use of, but again all that these references do is compete with one another, furthering the reader from a final moment of illumination.

Even the end point toward which the narrative moves has no real significance or meaning in the narrative in that, from the outset, the reader has been overwhelmed with atrocities, killings, shootings, and bombs. The final bomb in Carmincross is just one more in what has been a catalogue of destruction. If the purpose has been to numb his readers' response to that final outrage, then Kiely has certainly been successful. Daniel J. Casey, in acknowledging Mervyn Kavanagh's inability to explain the bomb, attempts to offer an upbeat interpretation by claiming that Kavanagh is ultimately a human and humane character, a representative of that 'indomitable spirit who stands steadfastly for life after the bomb' (*Contemporary Irish Novelists*, 26). Elmer Kennedy-Andrews also suggests that the novel is a 'poetic achievement' which highlights in a postmodernist fashion the 'bankruptcy of the totalising narratives of the past'. In other words, both Kavanagh and Kiely 'escape' history and are liberated from its determining grip:

> However, the potential for nightmare does not overhaul an unquenchable optimism, a deeply rooted confidence in humanity, and a sense of a fundamentally beneficent creative force. (Kennedy-Andrews, 101–2)

Certainly, emphasizing how the novel signals the uselessness of the traditional grand narratives of Ireland in the contemporary moment is important. Nonetheless, this desire to celebrate the humanity of Kavanagh ignores one crucial factor: Kavanagh leaves Ireland behind at the end of the novel to get on with his 'real' life back in America. His trip home has been an abject failure, compounded by the melodramatic fact that he was unable to prevent the bomb that killed his niece: the telephone warning came to his hotel room and he could not redirect it to the proper authorities quickly enough. This is, in itself, the true indication of the type of utter failure at work within the book. The violence in Northern Ireland is not to be confronted or understood; rather, it is to be escaped. The same is true, obviously, of Ireland's history. In the end Kavanagh does not 'escape' the narratives of Irish history, he is utterly overwhelmed by them.

If anger had been the predominant emotion in *Proxopera*, then in *Nothing Happens in Carmincross* it is one of hopelessness. In his review, Conor Cruise O'Brien taps into this bleak view of Ireland's predicament:

> It conveys better than any other book I can think of, a sense of the relationship of modern Catholic Ireland to its past, and the bearing of that relation on its future. Once you have taken it in, I think, you will realise that a paper agreement between a gentleman from Dublin and a lady from London is hardly likely to transform realities of life and death in Carmincross. (42–3)

Cruise O'Brien's mention of the Anglo-Irish Agreement highlights what is at stake in perpetuating a view of Ireland's future being predestined in this manner. The difficulty with this type of argument, then and now, is that it is far too determining and proscriptive. It suggests that there is 'nothing to be done' but accept some kind 'fate' or 'destiny' for the future. Or, perhaps, what is to be done is 'nothing', that is, leave the North of Ireland as it is. Daniel Casey says that *Nothing Happens in Carmincross* is a 'curiously apolitical novel' (*Contemporary Irish Novelists*, 26). Quite simply this is not the case. While Kiely/Kavanagh's version of Irish history does touch upon the other participants in the world of Northern Ireland – that is, the British and the Unionists – he focuses much more on the Nationalist side of the conflict. The implication is that it is Irish history alone that is to blame and it is Irish history that in some way must be forgotten or gotten over.

That the Anglo-Irish Agreement was signed in November of 1985 and that, now, we experience the realities of a peace process, however stuttering and faltering it may be, shows that action and change *is* possible, that Ireland's future need not be preordained. With this reality of the present moment in mind, it is possible to appreciate Benedict Kiely's *Nothing Happens in Carmincross* in a number of ways. The novel is a perfect illustration of one man's horror – perhaps a generation's horror – concerning the Troubles. The breakdown of formal representation itself is mirrored in the inadequacy of the response to the violence, where no effort is made to understand it in order that it may be brought to an end. As Neil Corcoran argues, 'The violence is … evoked in structures that attempt to command it in the discipline of form and order, but which nevertheless ironically register their own incapacity' (157). The novel cannot be seen as a solution or answer to violence. It is, rather, a debilitating product of that violence. Some critics are apt to confuse such a response with an actual remedy or antidote to the dilemma, when, in fact, all it does is reconfirm that dilemma.

What *Nothing Happens in Carmincross* embodies is not the beginning of a constructive response to the Troubles; instead, it demonstrates the end of a certain type of response, showing it to be totally ineffective. The breakdown in form within the novel reflects this situation, opening up a frightening vista of powerlessness in the face of Ireland's Troubles. Benedict Kiely and his character Mervyn Kavanagh's engagement with Irish history and Irish culture fails, given that they view that history and that culture as inimical to progress and to the future. Nevertheless, the novel does indicate – because of its failure – the absolute need for a more creative approach to Ireland's past and present that might begin to imagine the world, not as it is, but as it might be. It indicates the necessity for a language or a discourse or a form that can accommodate change and transformation rather than simply reflect stagnation and stasis. Only then can the future be fully grasped, with all its unknown potential and possibility.

WORKS CITED

Allen, Robert. 'Chronicle of a Mutilated Land'. *Irish Times* 27 Sept. 1985.

Benjamin, Walter. *The Arcades Project*. Trans. Howard Eiland and Kevin McLaughlin. Cambridge, Mass.: Belknap Press of Harvard UP, 2002.

Cahalan, James M. *The Irish Novel: A Critical History*. Dublin: Gill and Macmillan, 1988.

Casey, Daniel J. *Benedict Kiely*. Lewisburg: Bucknell UP, 1974.

—. 'Benedict Kiely'. *Contemporary Irish Novelists*. Ed. Rudiger Imhof. Tubingen: GNV, 1990. 25–39.

Casey, Kevin. 'The Return of the Native'. *Irish Times* 12 Sept. 1985.

Corcoran, Neil. *After Yeats and Joyce*. Oxford: Oxford UP, 1997.

Dunne, John. 'Prolixopera'. *Books Ireland* 99 (1985): 225–6.

Flower, Dean. Rev. of *Nothing Happens in Carmincross*, by Benedict Kiely. *Hudson Review* 39.2 (Summer 1986): 309–21.

Kennedy-Andrews, Elmer. *Fiction and the Northern Ireland Troubles since 1969: (de-) constructing the North*. Dublin: Four Courts Press, 2003.

Kiely, Benedict. *Nothing Happens in Carmincross*. London: Methuen, 1987.

Longley, Edna. 'Poetry in the Wars'. *Field Day Anthology of Irish Writing*, vol. 3. Ed. Seamus Deane et al. Derry: Field Day, 1991. 648–54.

Myers, James P., Jr., ed. *Writing Irish: Selected Interviews with Irish Writers from the Irish Literary Supplement*. Syracuse: Syracuse UP, 1999.

O'Brien, Conor Cruise. 'Blood on the Border'. *New York Review of Books* 8 May 1986: 42–3.

O'Brien, Darcy. 'Our Gain from Kiely's Sense of Loss'. *Irish Literary Supplement* 5.1 (Spring 1986): 33.

Pelaschair, Laura. *Writing the North: The Contemporary Novel in Northern Ireland*. Trieste: Edizoni Pamaso, 1998.

Critical reductionism and Bernard MacLaverty's *Cal*

RICHARD HASLAM

> As soon as literary study recognizes that its proper task is the understanding
> of texts, the scientific principle of 'once is never' (*einmal ist keinmal*) no longer
> applies. For texts present themselves as individuals, not as specimens. We must
> try to interpret them at first in accord with the concrete process whose results
> they are, and not in accord with an abstract rule, which itself cannot be estab-
> lished without an understanding of individual passages and works ... his-
> toricity is in fact a part of ... [the individual work's] ... particularity, so that
> the *only* approach that does full justice to the work of art is the one that allows
> us to see history in the work of art, not the one that shows us the work of art
> in history. (Szondi, 13)

The Northern Irish novelist and screenwriter Ronan Bennett has claimed that 'a striking paradox' accompanies the artistic representation of political conflict in the North
of Ireland (199). Though the 'Troubles' are underpinned by 'strongly held political loyalties', he argues, the 'mainstream artistic mediators of the conflict have tended to opt,
like the largely middle-class audience they serve, for an apolitical vision' (200). For
Bennett, the work of these artists is 'marked by aloofness, by "being above it all", by
self-conscious distance from the two proletarian tribes fighting out their bloody, pointless, atavistic war' (200). Because such writers tend not to become politically 'involved',
Bennett maintains, the Troubles are treated in most fiction, film, and television drama
output as 'an appalling human tragedy, devoid of political content' (201).[1]

Amongst the novels arraigned by Bennett is Bernard MacLaverty's *Cal* (1983),
which tells the story of Cal Mc Cluskey, a guilt-ridden, 19-year-old Catholic, living
on the dole in a 1970s Northern Irish town. The reader gradually learns that the
young man's guilt stems from his involvement as a getaway driver in the IRA assas-

---

1 Bennett's 'Don't mention the war' is a revised and extended version of an 'An Irish Answer', a newspaper arti-
cle that appeared shortly before the IRA's 1994 cessation of militancy. In his editorial introduction to *The Hurt
World*, an anthology of short stories about the Troubles, Michael Parker challenges the generalizing claims of
'An Irish Answer'. Parker argues that fiction by mainstream writers such as Mary Beckett ('A Belfast Woman'),
Anne Devlin ('Naming the Names'), and Bernard MacLaverty ('The Daily Woman') is far from apolitical and
does not shirk from 'showing the injustices and incomprehensions which gave rise to and sustained the vio-
lence' (6). See also Parker and Liam Harte's introduction to *Contemporary Irish Fiction* (5–6).

sination of a Protestant reserve policeman. Cal hopes that a relationship with Marcella Morton, the policeman's Catholic widow, will somehow alleviate his unhappiness. But their affair is short-lived, due to consequences arising from Cal's forsaking of the IRA, and the story ends with his arrest by the police. Over the two decades since its publication, *Cal* has been reproached by several (mainly Irish) critics for reasons akin to those advanced by Bennett. How accurate are the critiques of *Cal* that lament its supposedly 'apolitical' stance? To answer this question, one must assess the theoretical assumptions that gird (in more than one sense) the deprecatory readings of *Cal*. If these assumptions have led critics to inaccurate constructions, then the role of theory in Irish literary criticism needs to be re-evaluated.

In a survey of Troubles novels (including *Cal*), Bill Rolston judged, 'As far as these thrillers are concerned, there is no political cause in Ireland – it is violence for its own sake, partly racial, and thriving on a culture of bitterness' ('Sex and Violence', 28).[2] He elsewhere contended, 'Stuff that tries to be literature falls into the same cliches you find in thrillers: the psychotic republican, the poor soldier as piggy-in-the-middle, the daughter of the republican who falls in love with the British soldier' (quoted in Bennett, 202). Bennett similarly listed what he saw as 'a set of complacent conventions' at work in most 'serious fiction' about the Troubles:

> that it is an irrational and bloody slaughter without solution; that both sides, republican and loyalist, are as bad as each other; that normal, sensitive people do not get involved, or if they do, it is reluctantly or through intimidation, and as soon as they are in, they want to get out; that the British presence may at times be heavy-handed and blundering but at bottom it is well-intentioned and indispensable. (200–1)

In a 1995 essay, Eve Patten similarly discerned stereotypical features in 'Northern Irish fiction'; its 'two limiting trends', she claimed, were 'the continued grip of a realist mode' and an 'obligation to offer a consensual (and usually apolitical) liberal humanist comment on the predicament' (131). Patten included *Cal* among those Troubles novels in which

> Recourse to the juxtaposition of vulnerable individuals with an amorphous and superficially drawn terrorist presence has supplanted the novel's function of critique with a kind of literary compensation: consolatory images which provide for an unreflective but consensual response have obliterated the need

---

2 See also Rolston's 'Mothers, whores and villains'.

> to examine the complexity and ambiguity of social conflict, while the eleva-
> tion of individual sufferings has largely obscured the exploration of commu-
> nity, identity and motivation charted by a previous generation of writers. (132)

For Rolston and Bennett, then, *Cal* is deficient because it is steeped in cliché; for
Bennett and Patten, it also fails because of its allegedly apolitical, liberal humanist
stance. However, these critics, by subsuming *Cal* within generalizing accounts of the
purported characteristics of contemporary fiction about Northern Ireland, too often
ignore or misread crucial plot and character details and overlook or underestimate
questions of nuance. Many of the novel's vital particularities are thereby sacrificed for
the cause of a critical meta-narrative about the artistic inadequacy and/or ideological
delinquency of much Troubles fiction.[3]

   For example, Rolston's three Troubles clichés do not even apply to *Cal*: Skeffington
is not depicted as a psychopath, and there are no 'piggy in the middle' or enamoured-
of-the-daughter-of-a-republican soldiers.[4] Although Bennett's four 'complacent conventions' might appear more immediately pertinent, they too prove inadequate for
assessing the scope of MacLaverty's novel. As noted, the first 'convention' concerns
representations of the conflict as 'an irrational and bloody slaughter without solution'
(200). Bennett maintains that 'the recurrent metaphor' in Troubles fiction is 'the charnel house, the abattoir, in which the blood and the carcasses are laid out for inspec-
tion by the horrified reader' (202). As evidence, he cites three novels: *Cal*, Benedict
Kiely's *Proxopera* (1977), and Deirdre Madden's *Hidden Symptoms* (1986). But Bennett
is merging two separate metaphors ('the charnel house' and 'the abattoir') into one.
Since only *Cal* and *Hidden Symptoms* actually use the abattoir metaphor, two instances
have been amplified into evidence for *the* 'recurrent metaphor' of Troubles fiction.

   Nonetheless, given the horrific sectarian assassinations performed in Belfast in the
1970s by the so-called 'Shankill Butchers' (whose preferred instruments of execution
were abattoir knives and cleavers), an abattoir is at least a relevant allusion.[5] And even
though the abattoir is linked figuratively with political violence, the link is not only
with the IRA. Protestants comprise the abattoir's principal staff, and the Protestant

---

3 *Cal* has been critiqued severely on related, although not identical, grounds by Richard Kearney, Julian
Moynahan, and John Hill (although Hill's main focus is on the film adaptation of *Cal*). In '"Designed to cause
suffering"', I question many of their conclusions.   4 One's conviction of the accuracy of Rolston's interpretation is not helped by his ascription of the novel to *Michael* MacLaverty ('Sex and Violence', 27). Nonetheless,
in a spirit of self-critique and with twelve years of hindsight, MacLaverty conceded during a 1995 interview that
Cal's 'spectrum' of IRA characters ('the Skeffington figure who is ruthless and intelligent ... the Crilly figure
who is not too bright but active and will do things ... And, in the middle ... Cal, who is a kind of reasonable
individual') may have been too 'stereotyped' (González, 29).   5 On the Shankill Butchers and their weapons,
see Dillon, 49, 67.

preacher's drinking of blood straight from the freshly slaughtered animals (MacLaverty, *Cal,* 7–8) is every bit as metaphorical as Cal's reluctance to enter the abattoir (Bennett, 202). In fact, the novel depicts the ideology of loyalism much more negatively than republicanism: for example, the loyalist Cyril Dunlop argues, with respect to the 'war' against the IRA, that 'Hitler had the right idea' about dealing with his enemies (111). Bennett's second convention, which posits a fictional parity of (lack of) esteem in which 'both sides … are as bad as each other' (202), is thus inapplicable to *Cal.*

Part of Bennett's third convention decrees that if 'normal, sensitive people' do get 'involved' in the IRA they very soon 'want to get out' (201). Cal does want to get out, but (as I argue below) this desire is pervaded with dramatic irony. Bennett also refers to the convention that 'normal, sensitive people' only get involved 'reluctantly or through intimidation' (201). Cal does get involved with the IRA because of intimidation, but it is *loyalist,* not republican, intimidation. This is of crucial significance because it provides the novel with a considerably more complex political context.

Such a context is just what the novel's detractors have denied. As noted, Bennett and Patten claim that novels like *Cal* exhibit an 'apolitical' perspective, while Rolston maintains that such works suggest 'there is no political cause in Ireland' ('Sex and Violence', 28). These claims are manifestly incorrect because the novel establishes in detail a political milieu for the violence depicted. Cal and his father Shamie are the last Catholic family in a loyalist estate, and it is the threat of being burnt out of their house that leads, step by step, to Cal's involvement with the IRA (MacLaverty, *Cal,* 29–30). A similar cause-and-effect sequence is established through echoing phrases. While awaiting a possible petrol bomb through the window, Shamie remarks to Cal, 'Isn't it a terrible thing … that those bastards have us whispering in our own house' (28). After Cal has been savagely beaten by a gang of loyalist thugs, one of whose members had earlier been described as wearing a red, white, and blue scarf (14), the narrator describes how the 'national anthem came on the television over a picture of the Queen in full uniform seated on a black horse' (48). After snapping off the television 'without looking at it', Shamie observes (in a tone that MacLaverty chooses to leave unspecified), 'And they say it's a free bloody country' (48). Elements of Shamie's two observations are significantly echoed in Skeffington's comment on Bloody Sunday (when British soldiers opened fire on a Civil Rights march in Derry and killed fourteen Catholic civilians): 'And we were all Irishmen living in our own country. *They* were the trespassers' (67). By having Shamie's references to 'our own house' and 'a free bloody country' foreshadow Skeffington's references to 'our own country',

MacLaverty intensifies the narrative mood of living in a community under siege at both domestic and national levels.

Another example of this kind of political contextualization occurs after Cal has been beaten by the loyalist gang. He imagines a different scenario for his gang encounter, one in which he uses Shamie's gun to blow 'the big one's head apart' (47). Cal's fury prevents him from censoring this fantasy, even though he has experienced great guilt about participating in the killing of Morton. The brief sequence is significant because it highlights key questions posed by the novel: what are the ways in which the personal becomes – or always already is – political (and vice versa)? And where – if anywhere – are the spaces for ethical choice in the trajectory from apparent causes to real effects? These are questions to which the novel rightly provides no easy answers.

A further example of political contextualization occurs when Cal is cleaning out dung at the Morton farm. He recalls a sermon he had heard while a pupil at school, during the period 'when Civil Rights were on the go' (68). A priest had declared, 'For too long the Catholics of Ulster have been the hewers of wood and the drawers of water' (68; see also 104). Within a page, Dunlop informs Cal, 'I've nothing against Catholic people. It's the religion itself I don't like' (69). Dunlop then gives himself away further, by inadvertently revealing his involvement in the prejudicial firing of a Catholic labourer on the Morton farm, 'long before your so-called Civil Rights was ever heard of' (69–70). In this and many other passages, the novel accurately depicts the politics of communal proximity, or what Stephen Watt has called 'the minutiae of everyday … life in present-day Northern Ireland' (134). For instance, Cal recalls how, after standing '*for hours on end chatting* at the street corner' with Dunlop (my italics), Shamie would come home and declare:

> 'That Cyril Dunlop was in every Orange march that ever there was. And believe me, Cal, that Orange Order is rotten to the core. They wouldn't give you daylight if they could keep it off you'. (50)

As this shows, the novel is sensitive to the dissembling accommodations made by different social formations in Northern Ireland. MacLaverty's depiction thus challenges Eamonn Hughes's claim that the characters of *Cal* do not 'interact dynamically with the circumstantial reality of … violence' and that the author does not allow for 'the interplay of characters, form, and circumstances' (7). In addition, Stephen Watt (132–3) and Lauren Onkey (155–8) have astutely examined how MacLaverty deploys African-American allusions to underline 'Cal's feelings of political victimization' (Onkey 155). This tactic can usefully be compared with John Montague's short story

'The Cry' (1963), which also introduced the African-American analogy (81).[6] The specificity of *Cal*'s political contextualization thus confutes generalizing claims about 'an amorphous and superficially drawn terrorist presence', a failure 'to examine the complexity and ambiguity of social conflict', or an unwillingness to explore 'community, identity and motivation' (Patten 132).[7]

Although the grouping of Irish Troubles novels into various sub-genres may sometimes serve as a useful critical shorthand, sweeping classifications radically diminish our understanding of a work's complexities. Such reductionism can also be found in more highly theorized critiques. One of the sternest indictments of *Cal*'s supposed failings occurs in a forceful analysis by Joe Cleary, examining the politics of form in MacLaverty's novel, Neil Jordan's film *The Crying Game* (1992), and the novels of Joan Lingard. Drawing on the work of John Whyte, Cleary notes that the bulk of recent writing (academic, journalistic, and creative) on the Northern Ireland conflict adopts 'the "internal-conflict" model', an approach that

> perceives exogenous forces (whether imperialism or wider archipelagic processes of state formation) as being largely irrelevant to the conflict ... Instead, it diagnoses the sources of conflict in the intrinsic conditions and political culture of the region itself, and hence looks largely to internal solutions as well. (100–1)

Cleary claims that fictional texts shaped by the internal-conflict model concentrate 'on sectarianism while relegating state boundaries to the margins of the narrative'; as a result, he argues, they express 'a specific ideological conception of the Northern conflict ... premised on the assumption that the problem of sectarianism can be detached from the question of the existing state order in the British Isles' and that it can 'be settled ... without substantive overhaul of the current state order' (109). Thus, while the absence in *Cal* of any developed references to British (or Irish) state involvement in the conflict dispenses with the fourth of Ronan Bennett's aforementioned 'complacent conventions' – 'the British presence may at times be heavy-handed and blundering but at bottom it is well-intentioned and indispensable' (201) – the same absence constitutes a significant scotoma in the novel's range of vision.

6 'The Cry' skillfully recounts the operation of inter-communal accommodations during a pre-Troubles period: for example, in the wake of an RUC outrage, the protagonist's mother says of some of her Protestant neighbors, 'They're a bad lot ... But we have to live with them ... Why else did God put them there?' (77).   7 MacLaverty's cultural memory appears to fail him occasionally, for example with respect to the location of Matt Talbot's death and to the colours of umpires' flags for GAA games, as John Devitt has noted (52). However, Devitt's description of such minor slips as 'a grotesque mistake', as well as his claims that 'every Irish Catholic knows that Matt [*sic*] died in Granby Lane on his way to Mass in the nearby Dominican Church' and that 'the world and his wife know that a green flag is used' (52), are themselves culturally revealing.

However, while Cleary is persuasive about how an internal-conflict model can constrict fictional representation, his detailed reading of *Cal* is less convincing. For example, he argues that 'Marcella and the library [in which she works] both serve the process of domestication whereby Cal will come to reject the violently tribal world of sectarian working-class estates for the more humanising space of rural isolation, middle-class refinement and domestic sexuality' (123). But this neat antithesis dissolves if we recall that Skeffington is depicted as being distinctly middle-class: he lives 'in a big house with a gravelled driveway', a house that Cal finds 'luxurious, full of gilt mirrors and flock wallpaper' (MacLaverty, *Cal*, 63). Earlier, at a Gaelic football match, Skeffington remarks to Cal, 'There are not many aspects of *our* culture which interest Crilly' (40; italics mine). At the same time as he incorporates Cal within his (middle-class) conception of republican culture, Skeffington excludes Crilly, categorizing him merely as one of the 'useful … hard men and bandits' who 'punch the hole for *us* to get through later' (40; italics mine). Thus, the novel's working class / middle class distinction is evidently more complex than Cleary allows.

In addition, his assertion that the 'union' between Cal and Marcella 'is imagined … only in genocidal confessional terms (its consummation seems to require the absence of all of the Protestant characters from the scene)' is totally implausible (126). According to the novel, Marcella's in-laws are in Belfast (for an operation on Mr Morton's lungs), and the foreman Dunlop has gone home. The interpretation of their absences as some form of metaphorical genocide is an unconvincing extrapolation, resulting (it seems) from Cleary's use of a psychoanalytic interpretative model that blends notions from early and late Freud, René Girard, and Julia Kristeva. According to Cleary, *Cal* is one of those 'romance narratives – which often flaunt an Oedipal idiom that invites a psychoanalytic reading' (112; see also 122), and the fact that Cal dresses in the dead Morton's clothes before seducing Marcella 'links the earlier murder, in ostentatiously Freudian terms, to an unacknowledged desire to dispossess or displace Robert Morton' (122).

To acknowledge that MacLaverty is probably aware of certain Freudian concepts that have attained popular cultural status in the western world is one thing; to use as critical tools the discredited, pseudoscientific speculations of Freud and his epigones is quite another. Drawing on the extremely dubious authority of 'the Freudian version of the originary myth of the state' (127) – as revised by Kristeva – Cleary finds the 'cumulative political implication' of *Cal* to be

> that Northern Irish republican nationalists harbour a genocidal desire for an
> incestuous act of reunification and that, given the horrific implications of their

fantasy, they have no alternative but to renounce it and become reconciled
with the state against whose law they have transgressed. (128)

The novel does allude to genocide, but (as noted earlier) the allusion is made by the
loyalist Dunlop (110–11). Since the importance of familial motifs in Irish political
symbolism is manifest in the 1916 Proclamation, critical recourse to Freudianism is a
superfluous genuflection to what Frederick Crews has termed 'theoreticist apriorism'
(*Skeptical Engagements*, 173).[8]

Cleary's 'genocide' reading decodes *Cal* 'as a narrative of contrition whereby the
repentant Catholic nationalist guiltily offers himself up as a sacrifice to the proper
authority of the Northern Irish state against which he has offended' (127). The novel's
viewpoint, he continues, is shared by 'the revisionist interpretation of Irish politics'
(129):

> The questions that might well be addressed to *Cal*, however, and to the revi-
> sionist worldview, are whether reunification can only be imagined along such
> confessional lines, whether it must necessarily entail militarist violence or,
> indeed, whether the only alternative to militant struggle must be masochistic
> surrender to the Northern state as currently constituted. The paralysing
> ambivalence that informs *Cal* is ultimately derived from its own confessional
> conceptualisation of the conflict in Northern Ireland as a zero-sum game of
> all-or-nothing territorial control, the only imaginable outcome of which is
> either a resigned acceptance of the Northern state (whatever one's reservations)
> or its violent overthrow in the name of a United Ireland. That the conflict
> might be susceptible to some more emancipatory political resolution is some-
> thing the novel seems unable to imagine. (129)[9]

---

8 For a literary critic's perspective on the shortcomings of psychoanalysis and psychoanalytic criticism, see Crews;
Adolf Grünbaum has produced the most pertinent epistemological critiques. In addition to Frank Cioffi (who,
it must be noted, also critiques Grünbaum), see Esterson, Macmillan, Webster, and Wilcocks. In '"A race bashed
in the face"', I examine other applications and implications of psychoanalytic criticism for the analysis of Irish
culture.   9 'Revisionism' is a much debated term in Irish culture. According to Bennett, revisionist historians
argue that 'Irish nationalism is essentially reactionary, racist, irrelevant and founded on "pieties" and "myths"'
(203). Joe Cleary maintains that revisionism displaces 'interpretations of Irish history in terms of colonialism
and imperialism because these are deemed to lend themselves to dangerously populist and Anglophobic interpretations of the Irish past and, by extension, to lend credence to the militant republican campaign in the North'
(102). A qualified defense of revisionism can be found in the introduction and first chapter of Roy Foster's *Paddy
and Mr Punch* and in his *The Irish Story*; materials from the debate about revisionism and nationalism can be
found in the anthologies edited by Ciaran Brady, and by D. George Boyce and Alan O'Day.

Cleary's reference to conceptualizing the conflict as a 'zero-sum game' bears comparison with a passage in Padraig O'Malley's *Biting at the Grave*, describing the ideological fallout of the Hunger Strikes within Northern Ireland. According to O'Malley, 'protagonists defined their realities not in terms of their own interests but in terms of the interests of others, reducing every possibility to a zero-sum toss-up' – if 'your opponent was seen to gain, you were seen to lose' (213).[10] In terms of O'Malley's argument, then, *Cal* actually *exposes*, rather than succumbs to, a crucial dynamic in the political culture of Northern Ireland.

Because Cleary (like so many other critics of *Cal*) ignores the ironic potential of the novel's conclusion, in which Cal's mortification is probed rather than endorsed, he believes that the novel perpetuates rather than investigates a 'paralysing ambivalence'. But once we recognize that *Cal*'s final sentence is imbued with ironic shades, its depth-charge effect can be compared to the closing sentences of George Orwell's *1984*:

> The next morning, Christmas Eve, almost as if he expected it, the police arrived to arrest him and he stood in a dead man's Y-fronts listening to the charge, grateful that at last someone was going to beat him to within an inch of his life. (*Cal*, 154)

> But it was all right, everything was all right, the struggle was finished. He had won the victory over himself. He loved Big Brother. (Orwell, 309)

The conclusions to both novels imply that the predicament portrayed is to be resisted or at least interrogated.

One of the few critics to recognize the note of interrogation in *Cal*'s conclusion is Neil Corcoran, who has observed, 'The novel's power derives from its wavering perspectives: it is itself implicated in, and judgmental about the sado-masochistic cultural forms it anatomizes and inhabits. Its final sentence brilliantly yokes the implication and the judgement together' (156). 'What my characters say or do is not necessarily what I believe in', MacLaverty once observed, prefacing his remark with the word 'Obviously' (González, 36); however, many of his critics have obviously neglected to reflect upon this basic strategy of the fictional art.

Cal may be grateful that he is being given the chance to consummate his self-made, self-mortifying credo, which is inspired by the example of the Irish mystic,

10 O'Malley earlier describes how, in reaction to the Hunger Strikes, Northern Ireland Protestants interpreted their situation as one in which all things 'were reduced to zero-sum components' (189). Both Seamus Deane ('Wherever Green is Read', 101–2 and *Strange Country*, 29, 189–90, 193) and Declan Kiberd ('Elephant', 14–15 and *Inventing Ireland*, 643–4) have noted that, in recent decades, nationalism and revisionism have operated in Irish political culture as a kind of zero-sum dyad.

Matt Talbot, but it is far from clear that the novel endorses his masochism. As I have argued elsewhere, readers can just as legitimately infer that the novel presents – among many other things – a critique of the impoverished, theopolitical discourses of contemporary religious and political affiliation in the North of Ireland, a critique composed in the wake of the 1980 and 1981 Hunger Strikes.[11]

Evidence for an ironic reading of Cal's credo can be found in the scene in which Skeffington quotes from Patrick Pearse's poem 'The Mother'. After reading the poem's last line, 'My sons were faithful and they fought', Skeffington comments, 'Unlike you, Cahal'. When Cal replies, 'But it is not like 1916', Skeffington retorts, 'It wasn't like 1916 in 1916'. According to the narrator, 'a long silence' follows (66). For Declan Kiberd, this exchange in *Cal* concisely captures 'a dialectical tension between an action and its representation' (*Inventing Ireland*, 213). But a very specific form of 'dialectical tension' is at work here—the one known as irony. The same ironic tension operates between Cal's actions and the way he represents them to himself: through his self-mortifying credo, Cal is condemned (unknowingly) to mimic the figurations of an ideological system he has supposedly forsaken. The novel's ending is thus not at all 'consolatory' (Patten, 132).

Neither is it necessarily antagonistic to nationalism. When Cleary claims that *Cal*'s 'morphology' (that is, the construction of its narrative resolution) is 'hostile to Northern Irish nationalism, identifying it as a force to be purged' (136), he exaggerates. Morphology denotes both the branch of biology concerned with the forms of animals and plants and the branch of grammar that is concerned with the form of words. Through its concern with the word forms generated by religious and political discourse, *Cal*'s morphology is sometimes critical of aspects of Northern Irish republicanism (and loyalism), but it is not 'hostile'. By suggesting that *Cal* promotes the purging of Northern Irish nationalism, Cleary aligns the novel's inferred authorial stance with the genocidal allusions of the character Dunlop. This critical maneuver is a form of zero-sum exegesis, which dismisses the possibility of ironies, ambiguities, and contradictory evidence.

And there is much evidence in the novel to refute the thesis that it is anti-nationalist. For example, according to Cleary, when the Catholic protagonists of *Cal, The*

---

11 On theopolitics and the Hunger Strikes in relation to *Cal*, see my '"Designed to cause suffering"'. Instead of arguing that *Cal* is an allegory about the Hunger Strikes and therefore subordinating the novel to the determining context of the Hunger Strikes ('the work of art in history' [Szondi, 13]), I want to register how the Hunger Strikes resonate within the novel ('history in the work of art' [Szondi, 13]). However, as MacLaverty has acknowledged, there are also other, intentionally allegorical dimensions to his fiction (González, 25, 28–9). With regard to *Cal*'s implicit critique of religious and political masochism, see MacLaverty's (later) praise (González, 35) for Uta Ranke-Heinemann's *Eunuchs for the Kingdom of Heaven* (1988).

Crying Game, and the Joan Lingard novels renounce 'militant nationalism it is always to repudiate politics completely', and no alternatives 'such as working-class politics or constitutional nationalism or non-violent socialist republicanism or whatever' are considered (136–7). However, one plausible reason why Cal might not be ready to join a constitutional party is given in an early scene, when Skeffington observes sardonically:

> 'Others can ride on our coat-tails. The Gerry Fitts and the Humes. It's like a union. Some guys do all the work, others collect the pay rises without so much as a thank you. You have to steel yourself, Cal. Think of the issues, not the people. Think of an Ireland free of the Brits. Would we ever change it through the politicians?' (24)

Despite the fact that he has challenged Skeffington's earlier claims, Cal replies to this question with a simple 'No', and he subsequently agrees to be the driver for Crilly in a robbery to provide IRA funding. The second (and perhaps more pressing) reason why Cal cannot engage in constitutional politics is that for the latter half of the novel he is on the run, first from the IRA, and then from the RUC.

According to Cleary, the novel's plot traces 'a linear trajectory ... from murderous political activism to self-sacrificial resignation' and Cal (a 'reluctant accomplice') never becomes a militant nationalist 'because of any coherent critique of the Northern state or reasoned advocacy of a united Ireland, but rather because of an inchoate resentment against the existing order' (137). However, the novel makes it clear that, despite disowning militant nationalism, Cal nonetheless continues to hold nationalist beliefs. For example, almost three quarters of the way through the novel, Cal (perhaps optimistically) puts the case for a united Ireland to Dunlop (111). Later, when Morton's widow remarks, 'you never feel threatened in London' (118), Cal replies, 'That's because they're all over here wearing uniforms and beating the shite out of us' (118). This reply is all the more significant because the reader has already been given a detailed account of Morton's assassination and a vivid insight into Cal's consequent guilt (83–9). After Marcella accuses Cal of being 'very anti-British', he agrees, declaring both his desire for 'a united Ireland' (despite being unsure of 'the best way to go about it') and his belief that Ireland 'will only have a future when the British leave' (118). This observation, which certainly represents a good deal more than 'an inchoate resentment against the existing order' (Cleary, 137), challenges the claim that the novel 'seems unable to imagine' any other perspective on the conflict than 'either a resigned acceptance of the Northern state (whatever one's reservations) or its *violent* overthrow in the name of a United Ireland' (Cleary, 129; italics mine).

It is also significant that when Cal telephones the police about a fire bomb in the local library, he does not name names. His informing is a protest against the IRA labelling of the library as 'Government property' (MacLaverty, *Cal*, 145), which supposedly makes it a legitimate target; he is also protesting against the destruction of Marcella's workplace: 'He wanted to tell her that he had saved her precious library but knew it would be too complicated' (152).[12] There is no implication that the protagonist does not still desire a united Ireland in some form. When he earlier refers to people 'dying every day … in the name of … [a]n Ireland which never was and never would be' (83), Cal is rejecting a specific conceptualization of a united Ireland *achieved through violence*, rather than the principle of a united Ireland itself.

It is true that the origins of the theopolitical discourse shared by Cal, Skeffington, and Dunlop lie in the history of Ireland's domination by England. It is also true that MacLaverty's use of an internal-conflict model does diminish acknowledgement that England, with a monarch who is head of state and of the official church, has long subscribed to its own brand of theologized politics (particularly on those occasions when patriotic effusions are required). Nonetheless, MacLaverty's authorial perspective does not depend on what Ronan Bennett terms 'distance from the two sets of proletarian tribes fighting out their bloody, pointless, atavistic war' (200). Nor does *Cal* 'narrowly' imagine 'the conflict in terms of zero-sum struggles between state security forces and paramilitary subversives in which all other social agents are sidelined' (Cleary, 140). The novel identifies and exposes zero-sum perceptions, but it does not endorse them. *Cal* in no way takes 'the cycle of communal violence; the bitterly divided and segregated communities; the fact that most violence is concentrated in working-class ghettos' as '*unexamined* givens, as the circumstances that make Northern Ireland what it is' (Cleary, 141; italics mine). Instead, with an insider's understanding, the novel scrutinizes precisely the predicament described by Seamus Deane:

> The major communities in the North, Protestant and Catholic, unionist and nationalist, are compelled by the force of circumstances … to rehearse positions from which there is no exit … Each community feels that it is obliged … to retain the true faith, whether the faith of Irish republican nationalism, or of Protestant and British liberty. Each community sees the other as a threat to its existence. Each regards itself as … the preserver of basic principle, caricatured by its erstwhile allies and friends into a blind and benighted tribe. ('Introduction', 15–16)

12 Compare MacLaverty's novel, *Grace Notes* (1997), in which the narrator Catherine, a composer, reflects upon a dead IRA officer with whom she had attended primary school; she (ironically) ponders writing a piece for piano in his memory and calling it, '*On an Attempt to Burn Down the Linen Hall Library*' (84–6) – a reference to what was, in terms of propaganda, one of the IRA's less successful operations.

The languages of theologized politics and politicized theology, whether 'mystical Republicanism' (O'Malley, 26–7) or the 'God and Ulster' mind-set, are not the least of these forceful 'circumstances'. And the ironic unveiling of such circumstances in *Cal* is a very different matter from 'accepting the image of the North as fated' (Hughes, 7). If, as Glenn Patterson argues elsewhere in this volume, writers are called to recognize 'the crimes committed against language in any conflict' and 'to find ways of changing the vocabulary' (17), then MacLaverty should be viewed as an early and significant contributor to the piece-by-piece process of recognition and transformation that is intermittently occurring in the North / Northern Ireland / Ulster / Ireland / Great Britain / the United Kingdom.

However, the novel's contribution to that process has also been overlooked by more recent appraisals, which have built upon the work of Patten and Cleary. Elmer Kennedy-Andrews, in a wide-ranging and often thought-provoking survey of Troubles fiction since 1969, acknowledges that MacLaverty 'gives full weight to the economic deprivations and religious discrimination that one might expect to be powerful forces in politicizing a disaffected, identityless, alienated, Northern Irish Catholic youth like Cal' (89). But Kennedy-Andrews ignores the novel's dramatic ironies and concludes that MacLaverty, relying 'on a predictable plot and stereotyped emotional configurations … indulges an unhealthy appetite for victimage, passivity, and masochism' (91). John Devitt's pronouncements are even more rebarbative: *Cal*, we are told, is 'an extremely poor novel, unreliable in much of its cultural detail' (52); MacLaverty is an author whose 'pretensions are absurd' and who exhibits 'inept sleight of hand"' (52) and 'failures of imagination' (53). In pursuit of his theme, Devitt refers to Cleary's 'meticulous analysis of the novel's political incoherencies' (61), while Kennedy-Andrews claims that *Cal* provides 'a classic demonstration' of Patten's overall thesis (91).

If, however, as I have argued in this essay, the arguments advanced by Patten and Cleary contain serious limitations, at least with respect to their relevance for *Cal*, so too do those of Kennedy-Andrews and Devitt, which build upon the earlier analyses. And these various misreadings of *Cal* raise important methodological issues. Cleary states that the texts he analyzes must be read 'not simply as wholly isolated projects but as constituents of a larger narrative paradigm' (110). In this context, the concluding remarks of James Livesy and Stuart Murray's examination into connections between post-colonial theory and modern Irish culture are relevant: 'there is a tension at the heart of any post-colonial theory between its attention to the local and the specific and its desire to create a grand narrative of colonisation and liberation' (460).[13] I have sought to draw attention to 'the local' in *Cal* because such attention

13 On the need to recognize and renegotiate this tension, see also Howe, 129.

has been omitted by grander narratives of genre or critical theory. The omissions within these critical narratives lend a special irony to Rolston's remark that 'all generalizations [in works of fiction] reduce nuance' (quoted in Bennett, 8) and to Patten's claim that 'the "serious" Troubles novel has tended to universalize rather than particularize the situation, circumnavigating the Ulster condition through one-dimensional narrative and thematic limitation' (132). For critics too can generalize and universalize, and never more so than when they forget that 'texts present themselves as individuals, not as specimens' (Szondi, 13).

Of course, I in turn may be accused of leveling out the nuances of the various arguments I have analyzed. Achieving an equitable compromise between local and general perspectives is never easy, but we have to recognize the problem to remedy it. That is why I urge critics who wish to establish morphological correspondences to pay sufficient attention to specificities. Instead of the seductive reductionism of a zero-sum exegesis, we need a hermeneutic disposition, one that can minimize what Hans-Georg Gadamer has termed 'the abuse of method' (70).[14] Only then might we be able to rethink the way we bring method to work.

For this reason, a recent comment by Shaun Richards is especially interesting, since it was his *Writing Ireland* (1988), co-authored with David Cairns, that jump-started the drive to theorize Irish Studies. In a review of books on Irish drama, Richards concluded that the proliferation of 'a user-friendly cultural materialism glossed occasionally by Benjamin, Baudrillard and the other usual suspects' has led to 'a general sense of having entered a critical cul-de-sac' (107). Let me conclude by suggesting that the only way for Irish Studies critics to emerge from this cul-de-sac is to engage forthrightly with a challenge archly issued two centuries ago by Friedrich Schlegel: 'It is equally fatal for the mind to have a system and to have none. One must therefore decide to adopt both positions' (cited in Szondi, 61).[15]

---

14 As Gadamer notes, hermeneutics is an art, not a science – 'the art of employing methods where they belong, not where they don't belong' (70). Rather than being 'another doctrine of method', hermeneutics is 'a protection against the abuse of method, [but] not against methodicalness in general' (70).   15 Although I disagree with certain (but, certainly, not all) aspects of Joe Cleary's and Eve Patten's readings of *Cal*, I want to thank them for the courteous and insightful feedback they provided after the conference paper version of this essay was given. I also wish to thank John Devitt for his helpful input on the conference paper version. Des O'Rawe and Eamonn Hughes very kindly and insightfully responded to earlier drafts of this essay, as did my colleagues, Tom Brennan, Ann Green, April Lindner, Jo Alyson Parker, and Debbie Scott. Stimulating conversations with Terence Brown and with Brice Wachterhauser inspired me to pursue further some of the ideas in the paper, while Brian Cliff and Éibhear Walshe gave invaluable editing advice and encouragement throughout the process. Special thanks to Patricia Haslam for ameliorating the essay and other things.

WORKS CITED

Bennett, Ronan. 'Don't mention the war: Culture in Northern Ireland'. *Rethinking Northern Ireland: Culture, Ideology, Colonialism.* Ed. David Miller. Longman: London, 1998. 199–210.

Boyce, D. George and Alan O'Day, eds. *The Making of Modern Irish History: Revisionism and the Revisionist Controversy.* London: Routledge, 1996.

Brady, Ciaran, ed. *Interpreting Irish History: The Debate on Historical Revisionism, 1938–1994.* Dublin: Irish Academic Press, 1994.

Cairns, David and Shaun Richards. *Writing Ireland: Colonialism, Nationalism and Culture.* Manchester: Manchester UP, 1988.

Cioffi, Frank. *Freud and the Question of Pseudoscience.* Chicago: Open Court, 1998.

Cleary, Joe. *Literature, Partition and the Nation-State: Culture and Conflict in Ireland, Israel, and Palestine.* Cambridge: Cambridge UP, 2002.

Corcoran, Neil. *After Yeats and Joyce: Reading Modern Irish Literature.* New York: Oxford UP, 1997.

Crews, Frederick. *The Memory Wars: Freud's Legacy in Dispute.* New York: New York Review Books, 1995.

——. *Skeptical Engagements.* Oxford: Oxford UP, 1986.

——, ed. *Unauthorized Freud: Doubters Confront a Legend.* New York: Viking, 1998.

Deane, Seamus. 'Introduction'. *Nationalism, Colonialism, and Culture.* Terry Eagleton et al. Minneapolis: University of Minnesota Press, 1990. 3–19.

——. *Strange Country: Modernity and Nationhood in Irish Writing since 1790.* Oxford: Clarendon Press, 1997.

——. 'Wherever Green is Read'. *Revising the Rising.* Ed. Theo Dorgan and Máirín Ní Dhonnchadha. Derry: Field Day, 1991. 91–105.

Devitt, John. 'Two Films in a Blizzard of Intertexts'. *REA: A Journal of Religion, Education and the Arts* 3 (2003): 48–61.

Dillon, Martin. *The Shankill Butchers: A Case Study of Mass Murder.* 1989. London: Arrow, 1990.

Esterson, Allan. *Seductive Mirage: An Exploration of the Work of Sigmund Freud.* Chicago, Illinois: Open Court, 1993.

Foster, R. F. *The Irish Story: Telling Tales and Making It Up in Ireland.* London: Penguin, 2001.

——. *Paddy and Mr Punch: Connections in Irish and English History.* 1993. London: Penguin, 1995.

Gadamer, Hans-Georg. *Hans-Georg Gadamer on Education, Poetry, and History: Applied Hermeneutics.* Ed. D. Misgeld and G. Nicholson. Trans. Lawrence Schmidt and Monica Reuss. Albany: SUNY Press, 1992.

González, Rosa. '[Interview with] Bernard MacLaverty'. *Ireland in Writing: Interviews with Writers and Academics.* Ed. Jacqueline Hurtley et al. Amsterdam-Atlanta: Rodopi, 1998. 21–38.

Grunbäum, Adolf. *The Foundations of Psychoanalysis: A Philosophical Critique.* Berkeley: University of California Press, 1984.

——. *Validation in the Clinical Theory of Psychoanalysis: A Study in the Philosophy of Psychoanalysis.* Madison, Conn.: International Universities Press, 1993.

Harte, Liam, and Michael Parker, eds. *Contemporary Irish Fiction: Themes, Tropes, Theories.,* Basingstoke: Macmillan, 2000.

Haslam, Richard. '"Designed to cause suffering": *Cal* and the Politics of Imprisonment'. *Nua: Studies in Contemporary Irish Writing* III.1–2 (2002): 41–56.

——. '"A race bashed in the face": Imagining Ireland as a Damaged Child'. *Jouvert: a journal of post-colonial studies* 4.1 (Fall 1999): 28 paras. <http://social.chass.ncsu.edu/jouvert>.

Hill, John. 'Images of Violence'. *Cinema and Ireland*. Ed. Kevin Rockett, Luke Gibbons, and John Hill. 2nd ed. London: Routledge, 1988. 147–93.

Howe, Stephen. *Ireland and Empire: Colonial Legacies in Irish History and Culture*. Oxford: OUP, 2000.

Hughes, Eamonn. 'Introduction: Northern Ireland – border country'. *Culture and Politics in Northern Ireland, 1960–1990*. Ed. Eamonn Hughes. Milton Keynes: Open University Press, 1991. 1–12.

Kearney, Richard. 'The Nightmare of History'. *Irish Literary Supplement* 2.2 (1983): 24–5.

Kennedy-Andrews, Elmer. *Fiction and the Northern Ireland Troubles since 1969: (de-) constructing the North*. Dublin: Four Courts Press, 2003.

Kiberd, Declan. 'The Elephant of Revolutionary Forgetfulness'. *Revising the Rising*. Ed. Theo Dorgan and Máirín Ní Dhonnchadha. Derry: Field Day, 1991. 1–28.

—. *Inventing Ireland: The Literature of the Modern Nation*. London: Jonathan Cape, 1995.

Kiely, Benedict. *Proxopera*. London: Gollancz, 1977.

Livesy, James and Stuart Murray. 'Review article: Post-colonial theory and modern Irish Culture'. *Irish Historical Studies* XXX.119 (May 1997): 452–61.

MacLaverty, Bernard. *Cal*. 1983. London: Penguin, 1984.

—. *Grace Notes*. London: Jonathan Cape, 1997.

MacMillan, Malcolm. *Freud Evaluated: The Completed Arc*. New York: North-Holland, 1991.

Madden, Deirdre. *Hidden Symptoms*. Boston and New York: Atlantic Monthly Press, 1986.

Montague, John. 'The Cry'. *The Hurt World: Short Stories of the Troubles*. Ed. Michael Parker. Belfast: The Blackstaff Press, 1995. 64–91.

Moynahan, Julian. 'The Deceiving Conscience'. *New York Review of Books* XXI.2 (16 February 1984): 40–1.

O'Malley, Padraig. *Biting at the Grave: The Irish Hunger Strikes and the Politics of Despair*. Boston: Beacon Press, 1990.

Onkey, Lauren. 'Celtic Soul Brothers'. *Eire-Ireland* XXVIII.3 (Fall 1993): 147–158.

Orwell, George. *1984: a novel*. New York: Harcourt Brace and World, 1949.

Parker, Michael. 'Introduction'. *The Hurt World: Short Stories of the Troubles*. Ed. Michael Parker. Belfast: Blackstaff Press, 1995. 1–8.

Patten, Eve. 'Fiction in conflict: Northern Ireland's prodigal novelists'. *Peripheral Visions: Images of Nationhood in Contemporary British Fiction*. Ed. Ian A. Bell. Cardiff: University of Wales Press, 1995. 128–48.

Richards, Shaun. Rev. of '*Ireland's National Theaters ...* by Mary Trotter and *A Century of Irish Drama ...* by Stephen Watt et al.'. *Irish Studies Review* 10.1 (April 2002): 106–7.

Rolston, Bill. 'Mothers, whores and villains: images of women in novels of the Northern Ireland Conflict'. *Race and Class* 31.1 (1989): 41–57.

—. 'Sex and Violence: Images of Men in Novels of the Troubles'. *Irish Reporter* 14 (1994): 26–28.

Szondi, Peter. *On Textual Understanding and Other Essays*. Trans. Harvey Mendelsohn. Minneapolis: University of Minnesota Press, 1986.

Watt, Stephen. 'The Politics of Bernard MacLaverty's *Cal*'. *Eire-Ireland* XVIII. 3 (Fall 1993): 130–46.

Webster, Richard. *Why Freud Was Wrong: Sin, Science and Psychoanalysis*. New York: Basic Books, 1995.

Whyte, John. *Interpreting Northern Ireland*. Oxford: Clarendon Press, 1991.

Wilcocks, Robert. *Maelzel's Chess Player: Sigmund Freud and the Rhetoric of Deceit*. Lanham, Md: Rowan and Littlefield, 1994.

Politicizing the private: women writing the Troubles

JAYNE STEEL

Women writing the troubles. This field of study emerged from my earlier research about how British identity effects representations of the Provisional IRA in British film, fiction, and media. Not surprisingly, this earlier research involved the analyses of predominately male-authored texts that J. Bowyer Bell has dubbed 'Troubles Trash' (26). Such narratives about the conflict in the north of Ireland lend themselves to the thriller genre, to literary *realism*, to the public domain of men and war rather than the private domain of women and home. When women do make an appearance, they tend to conform to a series of stereotypes. These include the long-suffering domestic drudge, or, as Catherine Shannon notes, the repetition of clichéd figures churned out by 'the British tabloid press to portray northern women as passive victims of para-military mobsters or bomb-throwing viragoes and godmothers of hate' (241). Then there is the *femme fatal*, or '*vampira*', or the fantasy female who splices Eros with Thanatos to 'give the male reader a good time' by proxy (see Steel, 273–83). Shannon identifies another type, the 'sacrificial Mother Ireland' (251). She also explores how women writers such as Anne Devlin offer alternative sites for female identification. For instance, Shannon discusses Devlin's play *Ourselves Alone,* and asserts that Devlin 'refuses to consider the hunger-strikers unblemished heroes' while, at the same time, portraying a female character who 'rejects the whole republican enterprise by declaring her total indifference to the goal of Irish unity, and insists that British withdrawal will do nothing to liberate [women] from a life of service and sacrifice for their men' (251). This life of service and sacrifice repeated in fiction is often linked to the private *vis-à-vis* the home, where women *service* men and *sacrifice* female autonomy at both a sexual and a domestic level.

When it comes to Irish women and history, Margaret Ward notes how 'men have written women out of history' (4). 'Women are not', says Ward, 'seen as part of Irish history, and neither are the causes they fought for' (7). Bearing these points in mind, the following paper discusses four female-authored contemporary novels: *One by One in the Darkness,* by Deirdre Madden; *Shadows on Our Skin,* by Jennifer Johnston; *To Stay Alive,* by Linda Anderson; and *Give Them Stones,* by Mary Beckett. I follow a methodological approach that draws upon French feminism and cultural materialism in order to raise certain questions. For instance, I ask if Irish women writers can supply what Jean Elshtain calls 'an alternative to seeing the history of women as an unbroken tale of victimization' (226)? I consider whether, or not, the private and domestic can be politicized for a feminist agenda. I also debate the potential for women to gain sovereignty of the self, politicize the private, rewrite the body and history, and challenge patriarchal ideals about the nation that subordinate female identity and material realities to national identity.

French feminist theorists such as Julia Kristeva have, of course, 'deep suspicions of identity' as a fixed or singular concept and 'reject any idea of an *écriture feminine* that would be inherently feminine or female' (Sarup, 142; see also 133–45). As a form of writing available to male *and* female authors, for Kristeva, *écriture feminine* can 'develop a notion of signifying practice … that covers both the [phallocentric] symbolic order of rational language [the domain of realism] and the marginal, repressed feminine discourses of poetry, irrationality, art and so on' (Sarup, 141). Writing that draws upon fairy-tale, myth, the surreal, stream of consciousness, 'madness', the body, the uncanny, and female sexuality can all be included here (Sarup, 143). In terms of poetry, writing that utilizes devices such as rhythm and tone can unleash the repressed 'semiotic *chora*' which, in turn, can disrupt the symbolic order of language (Sarup 141). This theoretical approach also favours the dismantling of binary hierarchies, which tend to privilege one concept over another: 'male over female', 'voice over silence', 'presence over absence', 'logos over pathos', 'head over emotion', 'reality over fantasy' (Sarup, 141, 133). It seems to me that, while not abandoning realism or the material, these ideas from French feminism can usefully support a methodological strategy that offers an alternative form of discourse to literary realism, not to mention to repetitions of male-authored history and the social, which become so normalized that other views are neglected.

One by One in the Darkness concerns three sisters (Cate, Helen and Sally) whose childhood memories are steeped in the rural idyll of the domestic home. The importance of 'home' to the sisters is presented with the first word of the novel when Cate returns from London for a visit:

> *Home* was a huge sky; it was flat fields of poor land fringed with hawthorn and alder. It was birds in flight; it was columns of midges like smoke in a summer dusk. It was grey water; it was a mad wind; it was a solid stone house where the silence was uncanny. (1; emphasis mine)

A close reading of this extract shows how Madden's writing of the private and domestic resonates with *écriture feminine*. Home is not just a 'solid stone house', not just, like the male symbolic order, a structure. For Cate, home is also a natural space ('hawthorn and elder'), a free and fluid space ('huge sky, grey water'), an irrational space ('mad wind'), an anti-empirical space ('uncanny'), and a space that contains absence ('silence'). The prose style is also poetic – anaphoric repetitions of 'it was' supply the opening paragraph with a pulse, a rhythm, a semiotic *chora*.[1]

Cate is pregnant and works in London, Helen is a Belfast lawyer, and Sally is a schoolteacher who still lives at home with the sisters' widowed mother. Charlie, their father, is dead, having been murdered in error by Loyalist paramilitaries, a detail from the sisters' childhood not revealed until much later in the novel. In terms of structure, Madden's novel contains many flashbacks and, therefore, disrupts the despotic linearity adopted by historical meta-narratives. The use of flashbacks helps to create a more contingent past, a past that is constructed through memory. Unlike the ostensibly objective histories served up by the media (which, in fact, tell 'only part of the story'), subjective memory is shown to come closer to 'the essence of things' such as 'time', 'society', and the 'self' (Madden, 60).

In terms of the self, Madden's text also challenges ideas about the nation being the main signifier of identity. Unlike her iconic namesake, Kathleen Ni Houlihan, Cate changes the spelling of her name from ' "K" to a "C" ' because the former is 'too Irish' (4). Cate's struggle towards a more autonomous identity has been commented upon by Michael Parker, who notes how 'we discover Cate … examining in a mirror "the tiny invisible scar at her hairline" (Madden, 2), the result of an accident when she was six' (Parker, 95). For Parker, 'the scar figures as an originary emblem, lending the character "a sense of who she was, in a way that her reflection could not"' (95). What Parker means here is that Cate's scar symbolizes a '[self-]defined' identity based on agency, whereas the mirror returns just 'an image which "other people see"' (95).

Although the sisters appear to be very different, they also have much in common. All are 'single' and devoted to their dead father, a gentle, non-violent man who haunts their present through memory and dream. The sisters also share a tendency to veer from the male symbolic (language) to the female imaginary (colour, art, and chaos), a tendency that deconstructs the public and private. For example, Sally's work-space, her school-room, is both public (in term time, when populated with students) and private (in vacation time, when she is the sole occupant). Moreover, her school-room is a delightfully chaotic space that is cluttered with a childhood imagination. This childhood imagination portrays the domestic as a magical zone, displaying 'paintings of skewered mothers and fathers lolling outside vivid, pointed houses with trees like

1 Interestingly, this feminist discourse of memories, sisters, plus a whimsical, quasi-magical, rural past recalls Brian Friel's play *Dancing at Lughnasa*. This observation suggests that Kristeva has a point about male authors being able to write the feminine.

lollipops; [and a] list of words in colours written up in the colours themselves' (Madden, 137). As for Cate, she deconstructs the opposition between public and private to deal with the trauma of the past (her father's death) and the present (the ongoing political conflict). This happens when she imagines the building of a (public) monument to the dead that is akin to her memory of the (private) family home:

> She imagined a room, a perfectly square room. Three of its walls, unbroken by windows, would be covered by neat rows of names ... and the fourth wall would be nothing but a window. The whole structure would be built where the horizon was low, and the sky huge. It would be a place which afforded dignity to memory, where you could bring your anger as well as your grief. (149)

Geraldine Higgins has also highlighted this image, claiming that the 'imagined memorial ... suggests containment and interiority ... a window to the past ... and an opening out, gesturing towards the future' (158). Thus, Cate's feminine imagination succeeds in the unravelling of a number of hierarchical oppositions: public and private, past and future, past and present, inside and outside, confinement and freedom, culture and nature.

Even Helen, whose job as a solicitor conforms to the symbolic rule of law, has another side to her persona: in spite of her flat's 'clinical neatness', her bedroom is a wild zone of non-conformist chaos that displays 'a floor littered with unwashed coffee cups, compact discs, books and stray shoes' (Madden, 45). And, ironically, it is Helen the pragmatist who can 'slip into a fold in her mind somewhere between her dreams and her imagination. ... By the force of her imagination she would lift herself out of her bed, and pass through the roof of the house like a beam of light passing through water' (178–9).

The novel ends with Helen imagining a past she did not witness, her father's murder:

> she saw her father sitting at Lucy's kitchen table, drinking tea out of a blue mug. She could smell the smoke of his cigarette, even smell the familiar tweed of his jacket ... And then they shot him at point-blank range, blowing half his head away. (180–1)

Here she creates a more detailed, more poignant and, arguably, more 'real' narrative of the murder than the so-called facts reported in the male-dominated media. Further, her narrative also defies historical linearity by bringing the novel full circle back to 'the solid house [where] the silence was uncanny [and] one by one in the darkness, the sisters slept' (181).

Madden's novel is, of course, a material product of a specific historical moment. First published in Great Britain during 1996, the story was composed at the same time as the declaration of the first IRA ceasefire in August 1994. But the *One by One* narrative unfolds just prior to the ceasefire and the Good Friday Peace Agreement. Arguably, though, the reader at the time of the publication might have brought a certain optimism to the novel that was based on 'reality': the less volatile situation in the north of Ireland. This is not the case for Madden's fictive sisters. Their present day reality within the novel contains no ceasefire. Here, reality remains haunted by the conflict of the 1960s and 1970s, their father's death and the recorded history of the Troubles: the transcendental, symbolic, and masculine narratives of the historian and the media. Thus Madden inserts real events such as Bloody Friday (129) and real political figures such Bernadette Devlin (94). Yet the inclusion of these real events and real political figures cannot replicate the actual trauma experienced by those who suffered death or bereavement during the Troubles. Language is not sufficient to the job. And Madden seems to be aware of this failure of language when she implies how the real trauma of the 1960s, 1970s, and early 1980s (being shot, blown up, or beaten by paramilitaries) resists repetition through the symbolic order, through media-speak, or through the language of fiction. Indeed, the specious nature of the so-called facts, histories, or historiographies articulated by the media are summed up by Helen when she recalls the press reports about her father's murder: 'taking things and making stories about them … that's all it amounts to: making up stories out of a few facts, and presenting them as though that interpretation was the absolute truth' (50). Ultimately, *One by One* contests ideas about absolute truth. Fittingly, then, the novel ends with silence, with absence, with the notion that contingent versions of the past and constructed or imagined memories are just as valid, perhaps more valid, than ostensible facts.

Shifting location from the rural, Jennifer Johnston's *Shadows on our Skin* is set in a conflict-besieged 1970s Derry. Like Madden, Johnston deals with childhood, the Troubles, memory, the past, and the domestic. Published in 1977, *Shadows* is also a product of its turbulent time. The narrative concerns a young Catholic boy, Joe Logan, who is growing up in a war-weary city where Provo snipers and army raids are everyday events. Joe's Dad is a bed-ridden, whining invalid who exists on cigarettes, beer and rose-tinted memories of his 'heroic' Republican past, whereas Joe's Mum is a long suffering domestic drudge who works long hours. Lonely, unhappy, Joe befriends a young woman named Kathleen, a schoolteacher engaged to a British soldier. Not surprisingly, she asks Joe to keep her engagement a secret. Joe's older brother, Brendan, returns from London and becomes involved with the IRA. He also becomes involved with Kathleen. Joe is jealous of his brother's relationship with his special friend and, in a fit of temper, informs Brendan about her fiancé. This results in Kathleen receiving a punishment beating from the IRA – a result of Brendan's jealousy, not of his nationalism. The novel ends with Kathleen leaving Derry and, of course, Joe.

In spite of the dubious plot (Kathleen has moved from the South to Derry knowing that, because of her engagement to a British soldier, her life will almost certainly be in danger), does *Shadows* supply a gender politics that challenges more patriarchal representations of the Troubles? Well, like Madden's Cate, Johnston's Kathleen is no iconic Ni Houlihan – the latter would never be engaged to a British squaddie. Alternatively, then, Johnston's Kathleen might supply the reader with a female who is more subversive. After all, she is a bit of a free spirit: Joe calls her 'mad', while she admits to having 'no damn self-control' (Johnston, 31, 30) and, as noted by Ann Owens Weekes, thinks marriage is a 'mindless ritual' (198). Weekes also highlights the fact that Kathleen is an orphan and, therefore, free from familial ties (198). Further, although Kathleen is an English teacher, she rejects the rules of language and favours the semiotic *chora*, the pulses found in poetry and song:

> 'What do you teach?' [asks Joe]
> 'English … at least that's what I'm supposed to teach. In fact I find myself spouting out whatever happens to be in my mind that day. Do you know what is a past participle?'
> 'No'.
> 'Or a semi-colon?'
> 'No'.
> 'Or why you mustn't split an infinitive?'
> 'No. No. No'.
> 'Neither do I. Nor do I think it matters much'. (Johnston, 29)

Joe likewise struggles with the symbolic order. He finds Gaelic, a signifier of national identity, unfathomable and gets in trouble at school for writing poetry, a signifier of the imagination, instead of concentrating on 'equilateral triangle[s]' (29). Indeed, notions about language, and the inadequacy of language to construct the past or present, provide a theme for the novel. As one of Joe's poems informs us:

> Words run
> In and out of your mind

> Like children playing.
> And then
> When you really need them,
> Like children,
> They disappear. (200)

And Kathleen repeats Joe's viewpoint about language when she announces that 'words are aggravating, the way they hide on you when you need them most' (57).

Like Madden, Johnston focuses upon memories. However, the memories in *Shadows* are male, not female, and these memories belong to Joe's Dad, who languishes in a romanticized past of republican heroes, a past where he 'was … whole', suggesting he is now symbolically castrated (39). This feminization, or infantilization, of Joe's Dad is emphasized when he weeps for lost youth and reminisces about a past that is a 'fairy tale' (39). The phoney nature of his male memories is denounced by his wife, who recognizes that material inequalities are often ignored by male discourses:

> 'It's old buggers like you should be shot, with your talk and your singing of glory and heroes … women [are] scrubbing floors to keep home together because stupid, useless old men are sitting round gassing about freedom? Singing songs about heroes? Take your bloody fairy tales out of this house'.
> (171)

The novel was short-listed for the Booker Prize, yet, in an interview with Richard York, Johnston claims that *Shadows* is a 'wasted book' (York, 37). Johnston might have a point. Her text's realism slams the door on female agency – Kathleen and Joe's Mum cannot escape the social, political, and national. Instead of offering empowering alternatives to working-class oppression, Johnston merely repeats a roll call of stereotypes including the long-suffering domestic drudge, the female victim, and the bitter and old republican veteran (who is not unlike Eugene McCabe's hideous and invalid Irish republican mother in *Victims*). In *Shadows*, Irish women endure poverty, service men, forfeit material equality and suffer domestic as well as paramilitary violence for the 'good of the nation'. Yet, surely, this repetition of the realities of a patriarchal stranglehold functions to preserve the status quo when it is depicted as being inexorable. So, while I am not saying that these realities should be ignored, I am saying that they need to be subverted with alternative outcomes, or choices, for women.

With Linda Anderson's novel *To Stay Alive*, we have, arguably, a text bursting with gritty realism: poverty, bombs, bullets, sex and death. This Belfast narrative concerns three young working-class people: a married couple (Dan and Rosaleen) and a British soldier (Gerry) who hates army life. Dan is a medical student. He and Rosaleen have a baby and are dogged with the financial problems that are the catalyst for Dan's reluctant involvement with the IRA. The plot also involves a doomed affair between Rosaleen and Gerry.

Anderson offers a feminist text through a focus upon the body and the breaking down of binary oppositions. In terms of historical context, the body features profoundly. The narrative is set during 1979, a period when IRA prisoners were engaged in the 'dirty protest' prior to the hunger strikes. For Maud Ellmann, the 'dirty protest' signified an assertion of the self, because:

> Although [the prisoners'] world had been reduced to four cramped walls, within that tiny compass self was everywhere. Through the dirty protest, they were striving to reclaim their cells, just as they reclaimed their bodies through the hunger strike, for they cocooned themselves into their excremental signatures. (99–100)

Paradoxically, through their own agency, through the abjection of their own bodies, the prisoners reclaimed and, in turn, experienced greater psychological freedom than the working-class Catholics in Belfast. This is because, as Anderson shows, to be working-class and Catholic meant both physical and psychological imprisonment by poverty, a loss of agency, and a struggle to, quite literally, stay alive within a city where both male and female bodies were constantly threatened.

Accordingly, Christine St Peter notes that 'when Dan [is] lifted for interrogation and torture, his very body [is] the signifier of helplessness' (113). And Rosaleen shows she is aware of this when she observes how 'Dan's body was bent forward, rump jutting out like a female baboon inviting sexual entry' (Anderson, 162). St Peter comments upon how Dan's abjection, or objectification, results in a 'grotesque male version of gendered humiliation', a feminization of the male body (113). And this opposition between male and female is subverted, or deconstructed, throughout Anderson's text, in which men weep, tremble, and are shown as being passive sexual objects, whereas women, particularly Rosaleen, are capable of having profound sexual appetites and are intolerant of their roles as wives and mothers.

The novel also deconstructs more abstract oppositions. So, when Rosaleen copulates with Gerry in a graveyard, there is a blurring of sex (Eros) and death (Thanatos). Moreover, there is no easy distinction between good and bad, friend and foe: both the IRA and the British Army attract violent bigots as well as more compassionate types. In terms of the body and identity, Rosaleen provides the most interesting character upon whom to focus. Her female body is subjected to the threat of rape by the British Army and, if her affair is discovered, a punishment beating by the IRA. Indeed, Rosaleen speaks about a punishment beating which left the female victim with a 'wet slick of blood curling from the punctured womb' (47). Later on, and ironically, Rosaleen worries that she might be pregnant again:

> The period was so late. She hesitated, praying, willing the menstrual flow, then pressed her hand between her legs, withdrawing it smeared with blood.
> It was a reprieve. A sign. She could have a new life, scoured clean of everything that had happened. (94)

Here, the onset of Rosaleen's period signifies the opposite of the patriarchal and misogynistic notion that associates menstrual blood with the abject. Rosaleen's blood is, instead, liberating and cleansing.

However, through issues explored alongside the Troubles (motherhood, money, and marriage), *To Stay Alive* implies that the female body is subjected at various levels. For instance, although Rosaleen is sexually voracious, her body is appropriated by marriage, a fact made evident when, looking at Dan, she decides 'This is your country. And I'm your cunt' (44). She also argues against her friend's idea that Ireland, unlike China, is a 'free country':

> 'Free! Don't you realize it's the same here? The pressure is opposite, that's all. Priests and neighbours meddling into your sex lives, turning you into biddable little breeders'. (45)

'Biddable little breeders'? For working-class Catholic women like Rosaleen, the female body is not just subjected to threats of rape and punishment but also appropriated by patriarchy *vis-à-vis* marriage and religion. Critics such as Padraig O'Malley claim that, in terms of Rosaleen, Anderson's novel 'conveys an over-riding sense that there is no way out, no future, and no hope' (7). However, I am more convinced by St Peter's observation that Anderson 'refuses her readers any kind of closure' (114). This is because, although Anderson's female protagonist remains within Belfast and her unhappy marriage, St Peter notes, 'Rosaleen's fierce desire to stay alive in the face of so much death … marks a heroic struggle against the false forms of [male] heroism current in Belfast society' (114). Unlike *Shadows on Our Skin*, *To Stay Alive* leaves the reader with a sense that Irish women will never wholly capitulate to patriarchy.

The last novel I want to consider is Mary Beckett's *Give Them Stones* (1987). The narrative's protagonist is called Martha (a Biblical name that resonates with domestic duty). Martha is from a poor, Catholic, working-class Belfast family. Her story begins in the 1980s then shifts back to the 1940s and a childhood when, because of the Blitz, she is sent into the countryside. Here she lives for a number of years with two elderly female relatives, Bessie and Maggie, who teach her how to bake bread. Eventually, Martha inherits their small property, sells it, secretly places the money with a solicitor, and returns to Belfast. Here she marries Dermot because he owns a 'gas cooker' and she will be able to 'bake' (76). At this point, Martha claims her inheritance from the solicitor and uses the money to open a bakery within her marital home. Throughout the text, Martha's first person narrative voice supplies a haunting, lyrical tone, a feminine discourse similar to the one created by Madden, especially as the 1940s back-story is also set in rural Ireland.

Although, again like Madden, Beckett draws upon real historical events such as the General Strike, the Falls Road curfew, and Bloody Sunday, she writes these events from a female perspective that avoids a monolithic, phallocentric discourse and firmly places working-class Catholic women from the north of Ireland *and their stories* back into the Troubles. As noted by Megan Sullivan, the novel charts the main protagonist Martha's psychological journey from 'a national identity to a gender-based class politics' (42). This gender-based class politics revolves around the material, especially employment and wages. For instance, although Martha and Dermot have young children, Dermot keeps most of his wages. Yet Martha is able to prevent this material reality from inflicting deprivation upon herself and her children. Her self-sufficiency is a legacy from Bessie and Maggie, who have taught Martha to be 'in charge of [her] own life' and supplied her with the skills (bread-baking) as well as the financial means (the sale of the property) to act independently (Beckett, 54). Materially empowered by her late female relatives, Martha has enough money to launch her own bakery from home and thus create an autonomous, not to mention profitable, source of income: a female domain that is both a public space (the shop) and a private, domestic space (the home) (98).

This said, Martha's shift away from a national, male-dominated identity is not recognized by either the British Army or the IRA. For instance, when Martha refuses to serve British squaddies, the army assumes she is an IRA sympathizer, raids her bakery, and ruins her 'bins of flour' (127). Thus, a patriarchal imposition of national identity deprives Martha of her livelihood and the local working-class women of her cut-price bread. As Martha tells us, she 'never made much more than [she] needed for housekeeping' (148).

The incident with the British Army is later echoed by the Falls Road curfew of 1970 and Martha's sense of 'pride' when 'a whole army of women with bread and milk came marching down [the] streets … and pushed the soldiers away, shouting at them to go home to England and learn manners' (121). Both Martha and the female army are providers of bread not bullets; they are an active collective that, once mobilized, sustains rather than maims the working-class Catholic body. As suggested above, though, resistance to patriarchy gets punished. Hence, Martha is victimized by the British Army twice. The second incident happens after she has been given a record player by her sister and has acquired a taste for classical music. The music 'lift[s] her spirits', 'calms' her, provides her shop and her 'body' with a semiotic *chora* (134, 133). But her flights into the semiotic are thwarted when 'a crowd of … soldiers … open the door in the middle of the "1812"? Overture and sho[o]t a rubber bullet at [her] record player, knocking it off its shelf, breaking it in smithereens and fusing the electricity' (134). Note the humour here, though. In spite of her loss, Martha remains defiant and recounts the incident with subversive female laughter. However, it is not just the British army who inflicts male animosity on Irish female autonomy. So, when the IRA knee-cap a youth outside her shop, Martha protests by refusing to donate protection money. This defiance results in the IRA burning down her business and home, which leaves her feeling 'worthless [because] if [she is] not baking bread [she is] nobody and nothing' (147). Here, the bread that she baked and supplied to the women in her community appears to symbolize the female body, a quasi-transubstantiated body that gives the working-class bread (not 'stones'). Indeed, Sullivan touches upon these ideas concerning Martha and the female body when she writes:

> The [kneecapped] boy's body *stands in for* Martha's bakery, and Martha the worker and business owner is aligned with 'transgressive' youth … When the IRA threatens Martha's shop/body, it acknowledges that it knows the way in which a woman's body can be used by and for her; the IRA want to use Martha's body for its own purposes. (50)

The novel ends, paradoxically, with Martha and Declan receiving compensation from Sinn Féin and hoping to start over again. Whether or not Beckett's domestic heroine will be able to open a new business is left for the reader to decide. Finally, though, *Give Them Stones* suggests that national identity is patriarchal and that, like the Cuchulain myth which Martha criticizes because she does not 'believe all this "honour" stuff' (73), it reinforces a male-dominated history that takes no account of gender and class.

The four women writers that I have discussed have all, to a greater or lesser extent, challenged the ways in which the north of Ireland has been written as a male text. Such modern female voices enable both men and women from the north of Ireland to consider how politicising the private (the home, the body, the self) can provide a politically empowering feminist agenda.

WORKS CITED

Anderson, Linda. *To Stay Alive.* London: Bodley Head, 1984.

Beckett, Mary. *Give Them Stones.* London: Bloomsbury, 1987.

Bell, Bowyer J. 'The Troubles as Trash: Shadows of the Irish Gunman on an American Curtain'. *Hibernia* (20 January 1978): 26.

Ellmann, Maud. *The Hunger Artists: Starving, Writing and Imprisonment.* Cambridge, Mass: Harvard UP, 1993.

Elshtain, Jean Bethke. *Public Man, Private Woman: Woman in Social and Political Thought.* Oxford: Martin Robertson, 1981.

Friel, Brian. *Dancing at Lughnasa.* London: Faber and Faber, 1990.

Higgins, Geraldine. 'A Place to Bring Anger and Grief'. *Northern Narratives: Writing Ulster* 6 (1999): 143–59.

Johnston, Jennifer. *Shadows on Our Skin.* London: Review, 2002.

Madden, Deirdre. *One by One in the Darkness.* London: Faber and Faber, 1996.

McCabe, Eugene. *Victims.* London: Victor Gollancz, 1976.

O'Malley, Padraig. *The Uncivil Wars: Ireland Today.* London: Blackstaff, 1983.

Parker, Michael. 'Shadows on Glass: Self-Reflexivity in the Fiction of Deirdre Madden'. *Irish University Review* 30.1 (Spring/Summer 2000): 82–102.

St Peter, Christine. *Changing Ireland: Strategies in Contemporary Women's Fiction.* Basingstoke: Macmillan, 2000.

Sarup, Madan. *Jacques Lacan.* New York: Harvester Wheatsheaf, 1992.

Shannon, Catherine. 'The Woman Writer as Historical Witness'. *Women and Irish History.* Ed. Maryann Gialanella Valiulis and Mary O'Dowd. Belfast: Wolfhound Press, 1997. 239–335.

Steel, Jayne. '*Vampira:* Representations of the Irish Female Terrorist'. *Irish Studies Review* 6.3 (1998): 273–83.

Sullivan, Megan. *Women in Northern Ireland.* Gainesville: UP Florida, 1999.

Ward, Margaret. *The Missing Sex.* Dublin: Attic, 1991.

Weekes, Ann Owens. *Irish Women Writers: An Uncharted Tradition.* Lexington: University of Kentucky, 1990.

York, Richard. '"A Daft Way to Earn a Living": Jennifer Johnston and the Writer's Art: An Interview'. *Northern Narratives: Writing Ulster* 6 (1999): 29–47.

The Troubles and the family: women's theatre as political intervention

JOZEFINA KOMPORÁLY

The family and motherhood have constituted a major concern in Irish drama, the figure of the mother being traditionally perceived as a personification of the nation. Contemporary Irish women's drama, on the other hand, has mapped out an alternative pathway for the discussion of the maternal. This pathway has a looser connection to the personified nation, and exists as one option amongst other aspects of the feminine rather than as the ultimate role for women. This article centres on representative examples from the last two decades, hailing from both Northern Ireland and the Irish Republic: Christina Reid's *Tea in a China Cup* and *The Belle of Belfast City*, Anne Devlin's *Ourselves Alone* and *After Easter*, and Marina Carr's *Portia Coughlan*.

All of these plays focus on mothers and establish their lives as legitimate experiences for dramatic investigation. More specifically, they present mothers as individuals able to interrogate their maternal function and to relate to others in capacities beyond the confines of that function. Reid and Devlin not only concentrate on a single protagonist, like Carr does with Portia, but locate their characters in a community of women who share a female lineage or who are friends. Negotiating several decades in time, these playwrights bring together events from the lives of different generations, disregarding chronology and hence dislocating the linear sense of time and history. As Beth in Reid's *Tea in a China Cup* contends: 'I couldn't possibly remember it, I was only an infant, but I've heard that story and all the other family stories so often that I can remember and see clearly things that happened even before I was born' (10).[1]

Carr was born in the Republic, while Reid and Devlin were born in Belfast. To this day Carr continues to live and work in Ireland, whereas both Reid and Devlin have opted to live in Britain, mainly returning to Ireland for artistic inspiration. Despite this arrangement, their continued belief in the prevalence of Irish – as

---

1 *Tea in a China Cup*, directed by Leon Rubin, premiered at the Lyric Player's Theatre, Belfast on 9 November 1983. Following the positive reception of this play, a number of other works shortly emerged also focusing on the ways women in Northern Ireland experience their lives in the midst of the Troubles.

opposed to British or English – identity is emphatic, as Reid indicates: 'We [the Irish] don't speak English the same way [as the English do], our speech patterns are different, how we say things is different' (quoted in Herbert, 4). By bringing together representations of Irishness from both sides of the border and, indeed, of the Irish Sea, this article aims both to demonstrate that national identity is not merely a matter of geographical location and to interrogate the very necessity of categorization into dramatic genres. In particular, as I argue, the political theatre of all three playwrights destabilizes established genres by utilizing mythic and historical, public and private pathways to reinterpret the very nature of the conflict.

Christina Reid's work has primarily centred on interactions between mothers, daughters, and their extended families in the context of their respective religious and class allegiances. These women have largely been Northern Irish working-class Protestants – Reid's own background – though she also offers glimpses of the Catholic experience as observed from a Protestant perspective. Reid connects this preoccupation with female lineage back to her own childhood: 'All the greatest influences on my life were women – women talking, telling stories and jokes, all the sort of uninhibited humour that happens where there are no men about' (Campbell, 24–5). In fact, children, the young, and women are the key categories on which she concentrates, offering plausible investigations of their day-to-day lives in order to legitimize their experiences and to state that they are as important as any event in the public domain. Reid contends that she is concerned about the dominant tendency in contemporary Irish drama to 'portray Ireland through its violence', as all one consequently experiences 'are the Troubles and you lose sight of people' (McKenzie). It is to counteract this practice that she dwells on the domestic – generally involving several generations of women – and locates men on the periphery, showing them as incidental to women's lives, much as women would often have been represented in terms of men's lives until recently.[2] The key symbols in *Tea in a China Cup* eloquently sum up these two spheres: the portraits of men (fighting in the two World Wars and for the present British Army) represent the family's patriarchal line and its public facet, while the china cabinet connotes matrilineage and domestic history (Trotter, 173–4).

---

2 A number of mainstream Irish plays move away from the traditional male-dominated drama. Among others, Brian Friel's *Dancing at Lughnasa*, Frank McGuinness's *The Factory Girls*, and Tom Murphy's *Bailegangaire* focus on the world of women rather than men. In terms of critical reception, Anthony Roche and Christopher Murray acknowledge the significance of this major shift, yet also indicate that women's lives are represented from a male point of view in these plays. As Caroline Williams, administrator of the Glasshouse Theatre Company, noted in 1993, 'One of the difficulties … is that we are so used to men's images of men, and men's images of women on the stage, that a play written by a woman is regularly criticised for not complying with these norms' (quoted in O'Dwyer, 238).

This division between the public and the private as experienced by women is emphasized by Rose in *The Belle of Belfast City*: 'never forget that loyalty to one's immediate family will always take precedence over loyalty to the Unionist family' (Reid, 229).[3] This assertion also sums up Reid's artistic agenda in that she addresses 'the Troubles' without privileging political conflict. Reid's characters experience conflict with their families' beliefs, and dramatic tension is generally rooted in cross-generational confrontations that highlight the political and social transformations that have taken place over recent decades. Focusing on a range of younger characters in these conflicts, Reid explores the idea of accepting the past and moving beyond it to a new way of life, while 'neither embracing the martyrdom of foremothers nor validating the oppressive authority of forefathers' (McDonough, 191).

Reid often centres on such younger women to point out the striking similarities between Protestant and Catholic ideology, mainly in terms of women's status in society, and to question their assigned social roles. In *Tea in a China Cup*, she juxtaposes these views via the teenage friends Beth (a Protestant) and Theresa (a Catholic), both educated without any positive reference to their emerging femininity and raised in a total void with regard to transformations and experiences to come: 'We knew nothing. We found it impossible to get an accurate answer to anything relating to bodily functions' (28). Their impending womanhood is portrayed as a martyrdom of sorts, one that offers neither room for enjoyment nor potential for interrogation: 'It's just one of those things women have to put up with … there's a lot of things in life that women have to put up with, you'll find that out as you get older' (29).

'The public faces of the Protestant and Catholic paramilitaries', Reid has indicated, 'are all men. All the people who talk about religion and the Church are all men. The politicians are all men. Women are never the leaders, the faces, the voices. Ian Paisley and the Pope are basically in total agreement over what a woman's role in the home should be' (quoted in Herbert, 4). In a similar vein, Rose contends that the 'right-wing Protestant church is in total agreement with the right-wing Catholic Church on issues like divorce and abortion, on a woman's right to be anything other than a mother or a daughter or a sister or a wife' (Reid, 221). Such a constricted sense of femininity parallels the blame culture that women cultivate in considering themselves responsible for their men's behaviour and activities:

> Sarah: I sometimes think if I'd been a stronger sort of person, you know, took him in hand a bit more, that he'd of turned out all right. I was always too soft.

3 *The Belle of Belfast City* premiered at the Lyric Player's Theatre in Belfast on 3 May 1989.

Beth: You *do* blame yourself.

Sarah: A bit … mostly I blame his mother and his sisters for the way they
       spoilt him …

Beth: You, and all the other women like you. No matter what a man does
       wrong it's always some woman's fault, isn't it? (38)

Sarah's attitude, on the one hand, reflects a profound subservience of women's priorities to those of men, but, on the other, it also hints at a sense of agency, rooted in
the maternal, that connotes self-respect, maturity, and unchallenged power: 'Men
need looking after, like children, sure they never grow up' (38). As a further and much
more overt elaboration on the relationship between power, freedom, and the feminine, Reid contends that marriage and motherhood do not necessarily stifle women's
independent lives: Dolly gives birth to her second daughter, Rose, as late as her for-
ties, in the context of a very happy marital relationship with Jack; Beth and Theresa
continue their friendship irrespective of Beth's marriage; and Theresa does not marry
at all, fully aware that she is thus subverting traditional expectations.

At the core of Reid's theatre, therefore, lies a conflict of generations that contrasts
differing perspectives on most major aspects of life, including sexual politics. As
opposed to the young women who refuse patriarchal ideology, Reid's older women
(Sarah in *Tea in a China Cup* and Vi in *The Belle of the Belfast City*) not only acknowledge but accept the terms of their oppression, perpetuating sexual colonization. These
older women connote not only sexual but also moral and political complicity, in that
they support the status quo by producing and nurturing further offspring to continue the armed conflicts. For Vi, family solidarity is valued above all else, while the
two items Sarah holds the dearest are her china set (the symbol of her material wealth
and her upwardly mobile social ambitions) and her wedding ring (the indication of
her acceptance of religious and social norms).

Reid, however, also presents women as a source of vitality and creativity, as the
agents of genuine communication, humour, and caring. She does so mainly through
younger characters, like Beth and Theresa in *Tea in a China Cup* and Belle in *The
Belle of the Belfast City*, but also through Dolly, who is the embodiment of vitality
regardless of age. These figures are also the most transgressive, able to negotiate confining religious, national, and class boundaries and to argue for the viability of human
interaction as unrelated to the politics of location. Recalling her own childhood con-
tacts with women and children, Reid makes a case for the potential agelessness of all
women: 'they can talk like young girls at any age, and on their own are tremendously
uninhibited and bawdy – a side they would never show to men' (quoted in Roche,
234). While Reid generally allows her female protagonists to characterize themselves

and other women, she also includes male perspectives on women, the most extreme of which is that of Jack, Dolly's nephew and a Loyalist politician, who blends religious fanaticism with fierce misogyny: 'Women! Temptation! Deception! You're the instruments of the devil! The root of all evil!' (23).

In addition to mapping out a number of perspectives on women and various directions within the feminine, Reid also interrogates the limitations of gender roles as such and addresses the question of agency in relation to individual freedom. Some of the women, 'such as Janet, Rose and Belle, who place a high value on personal freedom, will move to England to live. The hardliners, who cling to traditional political and family values, will remain' (O'Dwyer, 241). Beyond this relatively straightforward geographical, political, and cultural opposition, however, most of Reid's female protagonists are often negotiating more than one alternative, trying to work their way through a range of options and ideologies. An illustrative example is Janet, whose spectacular transformation from total dependence on her brother and husband to a powerful reclamation of agency ('I want a life of my own. My own! Nobody else's!') starts from her unwillingness to be 'the sister of a devil and the wife of a saint' (Reid, 244, 208). A trip to London and the loss of her virginity after years of marriage initiate this irreversible change and make her aware of having been treated as 'a symbol rather than a person' by the men in her life (McDonough, 190). Beth similarly embarks on a new life following the death of her mother Sarah, when she is freed from 'the political straightjacket of loyalism and the gender straightjacket of her unhappy middle-class marriage' (O'Dwyer, 241). Though she does take one of Sarah's cherished Belleek cups into this new life – thus yielding to her mother's posthumous authority – she succeeds in imposing on herself a lesser emotional dependence and assertively confronting her past subservience: 'I've been my mother's daughter and … Stephen's wife … I've never been just me' (Reid, 50). The dilemma of these characters does not necessarily result from a central dichotomy any longer; instead, their quest is an exploration *par excellence,* like that of Belle, who was born in England of a mixed race partnership and who turns to Ireland not to oppose political Conservatism or Liberalism but to discover her roots, her maternal lineage.

Anne Devlin also investigates interpersonal relationships in a female lineage, focusing on reunions after periods of absence. Each of Devlin's two stage plays to date, *Ourselves Alone* (1986) and *After Easter* (1994), includes a central female triad, a microuniverse that negotiates a specific interaction with the broader spectrum of contemporary Irish and British society.[4] These female networks comprise both conventional

---

4 *Ourselves Alone,* directed by Simon Curtis, opened at the Liverpool Playhouse Studio on 24 October 1985. *After Easter,* directed by Michael Attenborough, opened on 18 May 1994 at the Other Place in Stratford.

and alternative family structures. The women are connected via bloodline – in *Ourselves Alone* Josie and Frieda are sisters and Donna is their brother's partner – but, more importantly, associated via friendship. In *After Easter* the protagonists are biological sisters, yet their family has been in dissolution for years as they have chosen alternative lifestyles and different geographical locations, reuniting only on the occasion of an ultimate disruption: their father's death. Nevertheless, for Devlin the family – be it unconventional and dysfunctional – is emblematic of the nation, and any revisiting of family links irrevocably triggers a re-examination of national and religious identity.

In both plays, Devlin examines the intricate ways in which women's lives connect to each other, simultaneously inviting and resisting the invasion of the private by the likes of politics (Republicanism) or religion (Catholicism). All the women express their political views – whether to oppose or support the ongoing conflict – yet their genuine concern is with the ways in which politics and history affect personal lives. Through this particular correlation between the personal and the political, Devlin conveys a feminist view with a slant: on the one hand, reclaiming the topic of political conflict for discussion in a new context, and, on the other, commanding a novel attention for a discussion of the feminine and the domestic in mainstream drama.

Utilizing sharp contrasts for dramatic effect, Devlin juxtaposes Josie's political commitment with Frieda's disinterest in ideology in *Ourselves Alone*, while she opposes Aoife's loyalty to her roots to Greta's and Helen's geographical and emotional distance from Ireland in *After Easter*. In this way, she foregrounds multiple options for women with regard to identity politics. Josie and Aoife can be read as representatives of what Devlin herself terms the 'traditional iconic point of view', whereas Frieda, Greta and Helen 'question that stance' through their alternative perspective (Cerquoni, 119–20). In an elaboration on the inherent aspects of the feminine, Devlin makes Donna, Greta, and Aoife the mothers, Josie the mistress, and Frieda and Helen the career women: three types representative 'of the three paths available at different stages of life' (Devlin quoted in Upton, 124).

In the view of several critics, however, even when Devlin depicts women as agents of political intervention they end up passive victims of a history that they cannot control. According to Susanne Greenhalgh, the avenues Devlin offers for Irish women only include exile or refuge into motherhood (166). Greenhalgh locates this comment in the broader historical context of Irish drama's distribution of political roles along the gender divide. Starting with Yeats's and Lady Gregory's feminization of Ireland as Cathleen ni Houlihan, political Irish drama (primarily male-authored) has centred on the male figure fighting for a vision of his country, aided by supportive yet passive female figures. The tasks ascribed to the latter typically include only the likes of banging garbage lids to signal the arrival of British troops, or making sandwiches and tea for the lads' (Shannon, 248), thus reinforcing the traditional view of women's social roles.

Devlin does investigate the route that associates women with passivity – she dwells on the sisters' aunt blinded by an exploding grenade and subsequently needing constant care – but she also interrogates this stereotype, most eloquently via Josie and Frieda. In fact, Devlin's work is a direct illustration of the claim that women 'have been left out [of the stories of political conflict] because … by not fitting existing discourses, they have not been recognized at all as socially relevant' (Aretxega, 4). Devlin's women simultaneously claim a space in domestic and public struggles, thereby undermining the traditional spheres of influence negotiated according to gender and launching new models of potential feminine behaviour.

Devlin's model is one of ambivalence with regard to women's involvement in the public political conflict, which allows immediate participation but also limited responsibility and, indeed, no support. Josie, for instance, is an active member of the IRA who not only works as a courier but also assumes executive roles, such as interviewing new members for the organization, and carries out terrorist activities, such as planting bombs. Yet she accepts being monitored by her father and lover from behind the scenes as she interviews, and is pleased when the bomb does not go off. When she finds herself pregnant by the man who betrayed her as a lover and who sold out their political cause to the British, she decides to keep the baby and finds refuge in the maternal, despite family advice to abort. This resolution, though in accordance with orthodox Catholicism, is an exclusive result of Josie's personal will, underpinned by her full awareness of the right to choose: 'It was my decision – it had nothing to do with you' (*Ourselves*, 78). While she accepts her father's protection, she again acts out of conviction rather than mere resignation, clearly refusing to re-live the life of her mother.

The poles that Devlin covers, as well as the characters she draws on in both plays, establish a correlation-*cum*-opposition between Ireland and Britain, replicating the playwright's own negotiation of belonging, emplacement, and displacement, of 'traveling between two zones' and being at 'the fault line' (Cerquoni, 122). Devlin's Catholic background and personal experience in Belfast's Andersontown shape the setting to *Ourselves Alone,* while her departure for England is replicated by Frieda's decision to abandon her family and leave Ireland behind. Presented as a funny and subversive character, Frieda exists at the margins of both family and society, uninvolved in the immediate political commitment that constitutes the others' *raison d'être*. Interested in seeing 'everybody's point of view' (38), Frieda 'plays jokes at things that are regarded as very sacred in political terms' (Cerquoni, 119), turning humour into a destabilizing factor.

In this sense she is set in constant opposition to Josie, not only as far as the two sisters' views on the Troubles are concerned but also regarding the negotiation of their personal lives. Josie's lovers are key figures in the IRA, connecting her political and personal affinities, whereas Frieda flirts with everyone, including such ideologically inappropriate cases as a member of the Worker's Party:

> Frieda: That's the only loyalty I know or care about. Loyalty to someone you love, regardless! I'd like to think if I loved someone I'd follow that person to hell! Politics has nothing to do with it!
>
> Josie: One day you will understand, when you come to the limits of what you do by yourself, that this is not dogma, that there are no personal differences between one person and another that are not political. (*Ourselves*, 23)

Thus, the very title of the play acquires polar connotations ranging from the Sinn Fein references, to the play's preoccupation with female networks and their resistance to violence, to Frieda's obsessive preoccupation with the sphere of the personal.

Frieda, however, also refuses to sing songs where 'the women are doormats', and protests against current and prospective gender roles: 'when there's a tricolour over the City Hall, Donna will still be making coffee for Joe Conran', she complains, 'and Josie will still be keeping house for her daddy, because it doesn't matter a damn whether the British are here or not' (13, 30). When she re-locates to England in order to come to grips with her identity, she does not commit an act of betrayal but instead actively attempts to re-assess her personal situation in relation to the political and social prerogatives of her community. Claiming to be 'anti-nationalist' – as 'nationalism is always the last resort for people who've failed to achieve anything else' (33) – she transfers her involvement from party political causes to the politics of art and performance in a gesture of contestation, refusing to follow the mould set out for Republican women. Frieda thus breaks with the constraints of the past and takes control of her own destiny, yet the play's challenge to tradition and patriarchy occurs only at the level of the individual, despite the resonance of these objections with major issues in sexual politics. As Carole-Anne Upton rightly argues, 'through a deconstruction of the prevailing orthodoxies of Catholic nationalism, [Devlin's] female characters may find self-fulfillment and even solidarity; but the assertion of the individual personality compromises the potential for collective action for social change' (122).

The individual versus the community is a central facet of Marina Carr's theatre as well. Despite the fact that she does not write from an immediate perspective on the

Troubles, her defining voice on matters of sexual politics is powerfully relevant to this discussion on Irishness, femininity, and contestation over the last few decades. Her dramatizations of gender roles, women's position in society, and the family command universal relevance by transcending both the terms of these conflicts and the confines of her plays' specific geographical settings. In this respect, Carr's work is archetypal – to the same extent that Reid's and Devlin's contributions are culturally and geographically specific – and she engages with the subconscious and the imaginary where the others emphasize the concrete. Yet, rather than simply prioritizing one over the other, Carr's work clearly communicates between the mythic and the real. While Reid and Devlin convey their interventions mainly in Standard English, Carr chooses to write in the dialect of the Irish Midlands, a region of her childhood and personal experiences.[5] In fact, she has set most of her plays to date in this universe of the Midlands, creating a unique environment that is rooted in realistic elements, and that only acquires a surreal tone subsequently.

Much as Greta is visited by the ghosts of her past in Devlin's *After Easter*, the thirtyish protagonist of *Portia Coughlan* is haunted by her spectral twin brother, dead for fifteen years. As Carr contends, 'in all of us there's a twin', and Portia's twin, 'an aspect of her that is dead or dying … is calling to her' (White, 10). Accordingly, the play interrogates such boundaries between the self and others, male and female, the living and the dead, past and present: 'When God was handin' out souls he must've got mine and Gabriel's mixed up, aither that or he gave us just the one between us' (Carr, 211). 'Writing from the unconscious' about such matters 'seems to be the best place … and the truest' for Carr, who acknowledges a strong Jungian influence on her effort to write more about 'things you can't understand than things you can' (quoted in Stephenson and Langridge, 148). From Carr's perspective, the ease with which she writes about these 'things' is a direct consequence of her worldview. Equally, however, it is also her way of pinpointing the rigidity of current conventions and expectations in the theatre, where the 'yardstick is frighteningly limited, and to work within those parameters is impossible for any writer who is on a journey, or who is trying to figure out what we're here for' (Murphy). In this way, she revisits the boundaries of acceptable dramatic practice and formulates a need for further and urgent public debate.

At the core of *Portia Coughlan* Carr places a quasi-incestuous bond between the protagonist and her brother, and a strong case of maternal rejection, directly resulting from that bond. For Portia, the bond with her brother constituted the ultimate

5 *Portia Coughlan* premiered at the Peacock Theatre in Dublin on 27 March 1996, directed by Garry Hynes. This production was based on Carr's initial version of the play, featuring much stronger dialect than the subsequently standardized language of the Faber edition of collected plays.

encounter and no other subsequent relationship has managed to measure up to it. Because Portia is driven by a powerful death instinct in the aftermath of her brother's drowning, every relationship she has since experienced represented nothing but a deferral of their imminent re-connection. Aware that this bond was a re-enactment of sorts of their parents' relationship, Portia is unable to find solace in her own family either: she is unable to maintain an adequate marital relationship or to experience maternal fulfillment. According to Carr, Portia 'doesn't know who she is and who she should be. The play is about her fight to stay in the world on her own terms' (White, 10). Fascinated by the genetic and social conditioning of the individual, Carr allows Portia to be both a victim and a heroine at the same time, testing the limits of her protagonist's ability to re-mould female destiny: 'I never wanted sons nor daughters and I never pretended otherwise to ya … But ya thought ya could woo me into motherhood. Well, it hasn't worked out, has it? You've your three sons now, so ya better mind them because I can't love them, Raphael. I'm just not able' (221).

As Carr indicates,

> The world should [not] assume that we are all natural mothers. And it does. It leads to very destructive living and thinking. … You're meant to adore your children at all times, and you're not meant to have a bad thought about them. That's fascism, … and it's elevating the child at the expense of the mother. It's like your life is not valid except in fulfilling this child's needs. What about your needs, desires, your wants, your problems? (quoted in Stephenson and Langridge, 150)

Though constantly afraid that she might harm her children – 'I'm afraid of them, Raphael! What I may do to them! … Ya think I don't wish I could be a natural mother, mindin' me children, playin' with them, doin' all the things a mother is supposed to do! When I look at my sons, Raphael, I see knives and accidents and terrible mutilations' (Carr, 233) – Portia refrains from hurting them. Unlike Hester, the 'Medea in the Midlands' in *By the Bog of Cats* (1998), then, Portia orients her pain and frustration on her own self, drowning in the river that once claimed her brother.

By portraying Portia as a woman who becomes aware that she cannot love her children – who, like the Mai, privileges passionate love instead of maternal love – Carr not only pushes the boundaries of acceptable subject matters available for dramatic representation, but also carries out an inquiry into currently available social and gender roles. In fact, *The Mai* (1995), *Portia Coughlan*, and *By the Bog of Cats* constitute a trilogy of sorts, all focusing on transgressive female figures who will not yield to social conventions simply on the grounds of tradition and expectations. Portia's rejection of mothering undermines any association between femininity, parenting, and caring, and it vehemently disrupts the pattern of committed mothers in Irish drama, a pattern with which both Reid and Devlin engage. Thus, Carr's seemingly non-political play re-politicizes the domestic by challenging age-old gender stereotypes (simultaneously tracing new avenues for both sexes with regard to parenting and sexuality), and re-inscribes the family as a legitimate site for major confrontation and tragedy.

Re-moulding the formats of the Irish family memory play and of male-centred discourse, Carr, Devlin, and Reid have successfully re-inscribed women's experience into the tradition of Irish theatre. All of the plays discussed here interrogate aspects of identity and belonging, address in detail the symbiosis between the personal and the political, and stage the re-configuration of current sexual politics. The authors dramatize in various forms the phenomenon of identification with a particular community, be it in terms of religion, politics, or gender, indicating both the inherent benefits and the limitations of solidarity. The structure of the traditional family is re-configured in all the plays – in the context of both public events and personal torment – as the playwrights problematise key aspects of family life: sisterhood, female lineage, and the mother-child bond. Thus, Reid, Devlin and Carr not only undermine any association of the familial with the idyllic, but also demonstrate that the family is a legitimate site of dramatic concern: it is symptomatic of the political struggle at large and, crucially, it contains the energies for psychological, social, and sexual regeneration.

WORKS CITED

Aretxega, Begoña. *Shattering Silence: Women, Nationalism and Political Subjectivity in Northern Ireland*. Princeton: Princeton UP, 1997.

Campbell, Kerry. 'Cuppas and Corpses: Kerry Campbell Talks to Christina Reid'. *Belfast Review* (Oct. 1983): 24-5.

Carr, Marina. *Plays 1: The Mai, Portia Coughlan, By the Bog of Cats*. London: Faber, 1999.

Cerquoni, Enrica. 'Anne Devlin in Conversation with Enrica Cerquoni'. *Theatre Talk: Voices of Irish Theatre Practitioners*. Ed. Lilian Chambers, Ger Fitzgibbon, Eamonn Jordan et al. Dublin: Carysfort Press, 2001. 107-23.

Devlin, Anne. *Ourselves Alone*. London: Faber, 1986.

—. *After Easter*. London: Faber, 1994.

Greenhalgh, Susanne. 'The Bomb in the Baby Carriage: Women and Terrorism in Contemporary Drama'. *Terrorism in Modern Drama*. Ed. John Orr and Dragan Klaic. Edinburgh UP, 1990. 160-83.

Herbert, Michael. 'Across the Great Divide'. *Irish Post* 22 Sept. 1990: 4.

McDonough, Carla J. '"I've Never Been Just Me": Rethinking Women's Positions in the Plays of Christina Reid'. Watt, Morgan, and Mustafa 179–92.

McKenzie, Susie. 'Interview with Christina Reid'. *Time Out* 10 Oct. 1984.

Murphy, Mike. 'Irish Writers in Conversation with Mike Murphy: Marina Carr'. http://www.rte.ie/radio/readingthefuture/carr.html. Site accessed 10 Mar. 2003.

Murray, Christopher. *Twentieth-Century Irish Drama: Mirror Up to Nation*. Manchester: Manchester UP, 1997.

O'Dwyer, Riana. 'The Imagination of Women's Reality: Christina Reid and Marina Carr'. *Theatre Stuff: Critical Essays on Contemporary Irish Theatre*. Ed. Eamonn Jordan. Dublin: Carysfort Press, 2000. 236–48.

Reid, Christina. *Plays: 1*. London: Methuen, 1997.

Roche, Anthony. *Contemporary Irish Drama from Beckett to McGuinness*. Dublin: Gill & Macmillan, 1994.

Shannon, Elizabeth. *I Am of Ireland: Women of the North Speak Out*. Amherst: University of Massachusetts Press, 1997.

Stephenson, Heidi, and Natasha Langridge. 'Marina Carr'. *Rage and Reason: Women Playwrights on Playwriting*. London: Methuen, 1997. 146–55.

Trotter, Mary. 'Translating Women into Irish History'. Watt, Morgan, and Mustafa 163–78.

Upton, Carole-Anne. 'Anne Devlin'. *Dictionary of Literary Biography, Volume 245: British and Irish Dramatists Since World War II*. 3rd series. Ed. John Bull. Detroit: Gale, 2001. 121–8.

Watt, Stephen, Eileen Morgan, and Shakir Mustafa, eds. *A Century of Irish Drama: Widening the Stage*. Bloomington: Indiana UP, 2000.

White, Victoria. 'Twin Speak: Victoria White Talks to Playwright Marina Carr'. *Irish Times* 19 Mar. 1996: 10.

The devil's own patriot games: the Troubles and the action movie

GERARDINE MEANEY

This chapter analyses the representation of the Troubles in the mainstream Hollywood action thriller of the 1990s. It focuses on two films, *Patriot Games* (Noyce, 1992) and *The Devil's Own* (Pakula, 1997), which elicited very different audience and media responses. *Patriot Games* initiated the highly successful series of films featuring CIA agent Jack Ryan, initially played by Harrison Ford, later by Ben Affleck. *The Devil's Own* recouped only $42.9 million of its $95 million budget at the US box office and was attacked by the British tabloid media as an apologia for the IRA. Between them the two films sketch the parameters within which the Troubles function in the Hollywood action thriller. *Patriot Games* established many of these parameters for the '90s. *The Devil's Own* exceeded them too early, having gone into production in the aftermath of the first IRA ceasefire in 1994, but released after the breakdown of that ceasefire and some months before its renewal in July 1997.

The purpose of this chapter is to locate the films within three interlocking contexts. The first is that of the development of the Hollywood action movie in the '90s. I will briefly sketch out the major critical debates in this area, focusing in particular on the analysis of male relationships of antagonism and friendship within the films and the reasons for the centrality of these relationships. I will draw on the paradigms established in the work of Cynthia Fuchs and Yvonne Tasker at the time, particularly on their analysis of the mediation of racial and social conflict in action films. The centrality of the family and kinship structures in action films dealing with Irish situations and characters will be analysed in the context of the genre's development and its treatment of masculine roles during the later '90s.

The second context of this discussion is provided by the 'Troubles' themselves and the political developments in the '90s. These problematised the 'myth of atavism' traced, for example, by Martin McLoone (65–9) through Hollywood representations of Ireland during this period. Here it is important to consider changing US policy and attitudes not only to Ireland itself, but also to the broader international scene. The third context is the study of ethnicity and neighbourhood in contemporary Hollywood, drawing on Diane Negra's insights into the role of ethnicity in stardom, but also applying models developed in recent work by Paula Massood and Vivian Sobchack, which use Bakhtin's theory of the narrative chronotope to analyse the construction of social, cultural, and geographical places in contemporary Hollywood film. One purpose of this discussion is to analyse the representation of Northern Ireland in the Hollywood action thriller in light of this recent work on the construction of a sense of place in film, and to integrate this analysis with the understanding of stardom, characterization, and the relationships between characters foregrounded in critical accounts of the action film. Massood and Sobchack are concerned with the narrative construction of very specific American places and genres. The contemporary action thriller raises the possibility that Hollywood's mapping of the relationship between its self and others' troubles is indicative of a global complex of chronotopes that constitutes a cultural map of a world view. While this map is projected onto US-Irish relations in the films under discussion here, it is motivated by a much broader set of international relations. In this final regard, the fundamental argument of this essay is that much more is at stake for Hollywood in 'Representing the Troubles' than the representation of Ireland itself. It proposes that Ireland serves a specific function in the re-imagining of the boundaries between heroes and villains in '90s' US popular culture and asks why Ireland is (still) able to perform this mythologizing task.

The action movie

Systematic analysis of the action movie over the last two decades is heavily indebted to the analysis of masculinity and the male body on screen that Steve Neale originated in his 1983 essay, 'Masculinity as Spectacle'. Neale's work took Laura Mulvey's analysis of the woman as object of the gaze and of the masculine structure of film spectatorship ('Visual Pleasure', 'Afterthoughts') as his starting point. His groundbreaking essay then developed the premise that the male body as object of the gaze stages a crisis within a structure of spectatorship predicated on the gendering of the gaze as masculine, the object of the gaze as feminine. Heavily Lacanian in its psychoanalytic underpinnings, Neale's argument set the discussion of spectacle firmly within the realm of the Imaginary, crucially marking narcissistic identification as a key component in the relationship between the male spectator and the action hero. The hero represents the Ego Ideal: in other words, in the relationship between the ego and its images, the male spectator finds in the male star the image he wishes to find in the mirror.

There is, however, a less obvious, but equally strong, counter current. For the ego will never reach its ideal and the male-to-male gaze is as voyeuristic in Neale's formulation as the male to female in Mulvey's. Both the classical Hollywood genres and the new action movies mediate the erotic gaze at the male object through spectacles of suffering, especially in scenes of combat. This applies to both male and female spectators. The fight scene in the much-analysed *Lethal Weapon* (Donner, 1987) is a typical case in point. Mel Gibson's character, Riggs, appears to stop in the middle of a knockdown fight to remove his shirt, thus presenting a more effective display of his musculature – and some relief from the tedium of the protracted fight scene, presumably, for Gibson's many female fans. As Neale acknowledged, if the male body as spectacle provokes a crisis of cinematic representation, it is a safely contained crisis. Suffering, torture and violence are visited upon these highly-paid and much worked-out male bodies to screen their status as objects of another's gaze. Hence a sado-masochistic dynamic is set up between hero and audience, and also within the relationships between men on screen. (Here Neale is close to the formulation of the interdependence of the homosocial and homosexual also outlined in the '80s by Eve Kosofsky Sedgwick.)

When a 1993 collection reproduced Neale's article as its springboard for a broader analysis of masculinity in cinema, the psychoanalytical critique of masculinity in cinema was modified by historical and social analysis. The interesting question, after all, was why the action movie was such a dominant trend in the cinema of the '80s that Yvonne Tasker could describe it as cinema of 'musculinity' (132). The post-Vietnam crisis of masculinity and of US self-confidence, combined with the emergence of the new right were important factors (Tasker, 91–108), but internal racial conflict was equally important. As Cynthia Fuchs so persuasively argued, action movies in the '80s consistently invoked a paradigm of male camaraderie, modelled on military camaraderie, which erased both the threat of the homoerotic and of racial conflict in the image of 'buddies' (194–212). 'The Buddy Politic' traces the displacement of sometimes nearly blatant homoeroticism in narrative emphasis on interracial partnership. Buddy action thrillers also displaced persistent paranoia about black male sexuality and miscegenation through an image of racial harmony without interracial sex. The imperative 'Look, black and white together', forestalled the question, 'Why are those men holding hands?' It is in this internal US context that the function of Irish characters and situations in the action thriller needs to be understood.

Racial tension was not the only imperative for change. Changing gender roles also generated significant mutations in the action genre in the '90s. Not the least of these was the advent of the female action hero, notably in the *Alien* and *Terminator* series of films. Action and masculinity were no longer synonymous. According to Yvonne Tasker, 'the emergence of action heroines into the mainstream has necessarily redefined the articulation of gender identity in the action picture' (33). One significant development was the increased tendency of the '90s action genre to figure the now apparently permanent crises of masculinity _and_ society in narrative terms as a crisis of fatherhood. The link between heroic status and regaining the role of good father emerged strongly in the _Die Hard_ series. Parallel to the built bodies and seriously deranged masculinities of the '80s genre, this series evolved another stereotype of masculinity: the wisecracking, flawed, ironic persona established by Bruce Willis. This latter stereotype is of course more in keeping in many respects with the traditionally understated hero of Hollywood thrillers, whose cunning, skill with weapons, and intelligence will always defeat the brute strength of an opponent. The smirk with which Willis played this role has spun off a continuing cycle of comedy thrillers, combining humour and special effects. The Hollywood action thrillers dealing with Northern Ireland do not belong to this strain, however, though it is obviously much beloved and aspired to by Irish directors and Irish film. (_Divorcing Jack_ [Caffrey, 1998] is an interesting variant on almost every convention of the genre in the context of pre-ceasefire Belfast.)[1]

Harrison Ford, who stars in both _Patriot Games_ and _The Devil's Own,_ made his reputation and originally established his star persona by playing the hero ironically in the _Star Wars_ and _Indiana Jones_ series. It is the aura of his other, later roles as the epitome of ordinary, male American decency that he brings to his two films dealing with the Troubles. This, and the downplaying of comic elements, is fundamentally connected to the centrality of family in these narratives and the seriousness with which the role of husband and father is treated. Ford's characters in these two films are the opposite of the always almost about to be divorced characters played by Willis. Strong family men with roles in law enforcement and government, the characters of Jack Ryan in _Patriot Games_ and Tom O'Meara in _The Devil's Own_ are poster boys for benevolent patriarchy. Since postmodern nostalgia became a major component in the Indiana Jones films, the action thriller has made 'how to be a man' an ironic question. This question can usually only be given emotional resonance by extending it to 'how to be a (good) father?' The predication of the national on the familial in these terms is central to both _Patriot Games_ and _The Devil's Own._

Family, nation, action

The video release and promotional poster for _Patriot Games_ carries its caption – 'Not for honour. Not for Country. For his wife and child' – above a still of Harrison Ford

---

1 The script was adapted by Colin Bateman from his novel of the same name.

pointing his gun directly at the onlooker, with a dark image of an eye peering out from a balaclava in the background, an image of rifle gun sights superimposed on both. The violence of Ryan is legitimated by his need to protect his family. The violence of Sean Bean's character, Miller, is also linked to familial ties, however. The contrast between the good nuclear American family and the dysfunctional Irish one is linked to the film's construction of their very different homes. An establishing opening shot identifies Ryan's home as a large and idyllic seaside family residence, respectable and prosperous. The voiceover features Ryan's telephone message, instructing the housekeeper on the care of the family's goldfish. This call and the shots of his empty home establish Jack Ryan's character: domesticated, responsible, a little humorous, and cutely forgetful. He is very concerned to protect his daughter from any unpleasantness that may occur as a result of an oversight on his part. In this case, the unpleasantness is death, which may already have overtaken the goldfish. Ironically of course, the threat of just this unpleasantness will overtake his family as a result of his intervention in a terrorist attack in London.

The film's London is a tourist cliché. The Ryans are shown ensconced in a luxurious hotel playing Monopoly with their young daughter. When she goes to bed, Jack's wife has champagne and candles delivered to the room as a prelude to the film's only love scene. Having established the hero as ideal husband and ideal father, the film immediately cuts from the Ryans' bedroom to Ryan in his role as senior CIA man addressing the British military on their mutual role in the new world order. The specific context is the aftermath of the Cold War:

> We have all watched with a sense of awe the protean events which have taken place in Moscow and the Republics and the enormous changes resulting from these events. In this volatile climate then I conclude we can only speculate about the future of Soviet fleet development and deployment.

Ryan's speech does several things. It presents our hero as a spokesperson for the United States and, indeed, as its embodiment. It locates the film in relation to the international political scene in a way which echoes the publicity's elision of Ireland into terrorism. It also reminds us why Jack Ryan is engaging with the Troubles in the first place: the horrible dilemmas presented to thriller writers and to Hollywood studios by the redundancy of the good old Cold War plots. The Russians were not coming, not ever again, and *Patriot Games* is part of a transition towards different kinds of plots, in which the new bad guys are terrorists who, however marginalized and misled, combine technological resources and military cunning. This new threat is just as much a menace to the United States as the old enemy.

The sequence following Ryan's speech intercuts scenes of his wife and daughter doing tourist London with a dissident republican cell planning an attack on yet another family unit, this time a neatly nuclear constituent grouping of the royal family. The sequence establishes a strong contrast between right and wrong family values. The dominant family relationship between the IRA men in *Patriot Games* is brotherhood. Excessive desire for vengeance on Miller's part scarcely needs to be attributed to guilt for involving his 'little brother' in the fatal attack. Their relationship is implicitly coded as diseased, introduced as it is by the handing on of the gun from older to younger brother. The opposite of the Ryans' fertile relationship, this family is constituted by a deathly male-to-male bond.

In the '90s the terrorist attacks carried out on US soil, such as the Unabomber attacks and the Oklahoma City Bombing in 1995, were predominantly by internal dissident groupings and individuals. Hollywood movies occasionally mirrored this, as in *Arlington Road* (Pellingham, 1999) for example, but this did not become a major trend. The equation of the foreign and the terrible continued to dominate the popular imagination. The Irish terrorists who feature in *Patriot Games* and *The Devil's Own,* however, do register the cultural impact of these home-grown terrorists. Part of the function of their white foreignness is both to acknowledge and exploit the anxiety that the terrorist is not immediately identifiable by his skin colour or strangeness. The Irish as terrorists keep the new threat at a safe distance and appropriately foreign: they might look like regular guys, but they are from a very different place. The ideas of place as a determinant of character and of origin as destiny run through both films, though the themes are very differently inflected. (While Northern Ireland is scarcely differentiated from any other terrorist origin in *Patriot Games*, the narrative implies that an excess of memory and attachment to the past is a crucial component in Miller's madness.)

The promotional poster and the video blurb for *Patriot Games* never mention the Troubles or Ireland, eliding them in references to 'lethal terrorist action' and 'a radical terrorist group'. Here it is Ireland's metonymic relation to terrorism that gives it its place in the narrative. That relation requires some examination. The Irish terrorist is both the same and different, white and foreign. He lends himself to the paranoid thriller because he can hide so easily, looking just like us, having no particular quarrel with the United States as such. In *Patriot Games*, the fact that this terrorist turns to an American target is motivated by revenge for his brother's shooting, with his obsessive pursuit of Ryan and his family in the second half of the film closer to the conventions of psychotic killer and stalker narratives. *Patriot Games'* fusion of the political and serial killer variants of the thriller genre makes a political point: terrorism is merely a particularly crazy variant of criminality. Stemming from excessive devotion to the ties of masculine kinship, its causes are located in the familial and are symptomatic of individual dysfunction. A causal framework in which terrorism can be investigated as a symptom of broader dysfunctions of social, political, regional, or global relations is unimaginable within the conventions of characterization and narrative deployed in *Patriot Games*.

Normal people in an abnormal situation?

Released five years later, *The Devil's Own* configures the relationship of family, nationality, and fatality differently. Its opening sequence features the brutal disruption of both family life and a traditional chronotope of 'Ireland'. Before the action starts, so to speak, in a pre-credit sequence we see a small boy helping his fisherman father on their boat, returning home to a scenic rural home presented as nurturing and warm. A fire blazes in the grate as the mother dishes up dinner and the family talk about their day seated around a circular table. There is a sudden jarring cut to a loyalist gunman, who literally breaks the family circle, shooting the father. The scene ends with an extreme close-up of the little boy's eyes, which fades to a grainy close up of the eyes of his adult self. The rest of the credits roll over this picture, which a voiceover identifies as Frankie the Angel, proceeding to list the number of British soldiers, RUC officers, and loyalist paramilitaries whom he has killed. The cut from Frankie's eyes shows a military briefing room which features both Frankie's picture and the sinister owner of the voice identifying him as a target for a military capture operation. The immediate cut from this room to a group of boys playing football in the streets of Belfast indicates a game is afoot and also reinforces the motif of children caught up in violence. Significantly, it is only at this point, when we cut to the streets of Belfast in 1992, that a caption is deemed necessary, identifying the place and the time. The run-down and militarized streets of Belfast are in strong contrast to the rural idyll in which the boy Frankie was introduced. Indeed they represent a chronotope of Irish place neither as firmly established nor as recognisable as the rural one, which, with its landscape dominated by mountains and isolated homes, needed no captions. 'Belfast, 1992' is the opposite of the scenic Irish landscape which has featured so persistently in films set in Ireland since the silent era. Interestingly, Frankie's escape from the gun battle in a ruined house (where the army ambushers are themselves ambushed by the IRA) involves his disappearance into foliage at the end of the overgrown garden. Nature at this point seems to be his preserve.

In telling the story of how Frankie became a gunman and of what motivates his mission in New York, *The Devil's Own* attempts to restore history to the myth of terrorism. The terrorist is a protagonist in his own story, not just a projection of another's fears. 'We're normal people in an abnormal situation, fighting a disgusting ugly war which you can't understand because you haven't lived it', Frankie later tells O'Meara. The film, despite the assumptions of condemnatory tabloids on its release, resolutely endorses O'Meara's denunciation of Frankie's actions, telling him he is only ensuring that other eight year olds will see their fathers die. The film also affords Frankie ample dialogue space to blame the British government for its failures in Northern Ireland, however. At least some of the tabloid fervour was a reaction to the casting: having Brad Pitt in the role of the IRA man indicates from the start that this is a very different characterization than the one afforded to Miller in *Patriot Games*. There the little-known Sean Bean cannot possibly counter the moral authority of the A-list Ford. In *The Devil's Own,* two Hollywood leading men are pitted against each other, representing different generations and types of hero, but both with the looks, profiles, and salaries of American heroes. It was not surprising that casting Pitt as Frankie would evoke resentment of the film's representation of the IRA in the British media. The breakdown of the ceasefire also provoked the actor to distance himself from the film by describing it as 'irresponsible' in a *Newsweek* interview, which generated another controversy in the US media (Giles, 50).

Yet *The Devil's Own* shares *Patriot Games'* grounding of character development and motivation in the familial and the personal. Numerous shots of children playing in the build-up to the first gun battle and one of a mother trying to shield her small children from gunfire in a recess establish that children are not safe in Belfast. When Frankie, now calling himself Rory, arrives at Tom O'Meara's house in New York, it is as if he has returned to the idyllic familial space of his childhood home. A scene where he shares a meal with the O'Meara family reinforces this, echoing the earlier scene of his own family around the table. A son who has lost his father, Frankie/Rory meets in Tom O'Meara a father who has no sons, though he does have three daughters. Ethnic identity here is almost indistinguishable from the familial. It is also linked to a re-assertion of masculinity: Tom initially tells the young Irishman that it's good to have someone else in the house who pees standing up. When Tom's wife sends him out for milk, he diverts to a neighbourhood bar with Frankie/Rory. Here they exchange insults with a group of local Italian-Americans and beat them at pool, with rousing Irish traditional music on the soundtrack. (When the Italians challenge them to the pool game, Tom tells the barman to throw the milk in the cooler.) This triumphant, macho ethnicity is utterly discredited in the film in narrative terms, but its easy conviviality is never matched by the complex, negotiated set of relationships between colleagues that characterize Tom's role as a policeman. Rory tells Tom of the murder of his own father, a story which the hard-bitten cop finds both distressing and moving, and one which invokes in him a fatherly protectiveness towards the younger man that ultimately survives even Rory's endangerment of O'Meara's actual family.

Rory's integration into that family seems complete on the day when he participates in celebrating their daughter's confirmation. Accompanying them to church, the camera focuses on Rory's troubled face as the priest repeats the tenets of the Catholic faith. The family party after the confirmation, complete with fiddlers, reprises all of the clichés of Irish ethnic identity and simultaneously marks the high point of Rory's integration into the O'Meara household. It is preceded, however, by scenes of his continued activities acquiring arms for the IRA, and succeeded by one of his romantic meeting with a young Irishwoman who is similarly involved. It is she who asks him if he ever feels guilty about what they are doing and elicits the response, 'Everyone has ghosts, no one's innocent in this situation'. This metaphor of haunting recurs in the film. Frankie is haunted by the death of his father. He himself is a spectre of a history elsewhere which haunts not just Irish-Americans, but all forms of ethnicity and even the apparatus of law and order itself. Not only is Tom O'Meara a policeman, but the prominent Irish-American who has knowingly persuaded him to take in an IRA gun-runner is a local judge.

Partners, fathers and sons

The Devil's Own's exploration of Irish-American identity is grounded, through a series of scenes portraying Tom's working days on the streets of New York, in a web of inter-racial and inter-ethnic relationships characterized by misunderstanding and potential violence. Initially O'Meara's police role in this context is co-extensive with his paternal one at home. We see him intervene in a commonsensical and compassionate way when a rookie cop mistakenly chases a young African-American. O'Meara's relationship with his Hispanic partner, Eddie Diaz (played by Rubén Blades), is also initially a classic buddy partnership, until the latter shoots a suspect. The morally upright O'Meara reports his friend: 'We're in the police business, Eddie, not the revenge business'. This rupture in what had been a co-equal partnership makes O'Meara even more open to and dependent on the paternal relationship he develops with Frankie/Rory. Yet when a group of gunmen raid O'Meara's house and hold his wife hostage while they search for Frankie/Rory's IRA arms money, it is to his former partner that O'Meara turns for help. The multicultural camaraderie of the streets which binds these two proves more reliable than either the ethnic and familial ties that link Tom to Frankie/Rory, *or* the codified world of 'the force' and the law. Tom needs his old buddy when his family is threatened. When Frankie/Rory kills Eddie while escaping custody, O'Meara's temporary prioritizing of ethnic affiliation modelled on familial (father-son) relations over equal partnership based on common experience proves to be fatal for his partner. It also isolates Tom and pushes him into an oppositional relation with the system that had previously defined his identity. Sloan, the British agent working with the FBI to apprehend Frankie/Rory, asks O'Meara 'What exactly is your relationship with this terrorist?', commenting, 'You *are* Irish.' O'Meara responds, 'So is Cardinal O'Connor', and refuses to co-operate with the investigation. This British-American co-operative venture is condemned by Ryan, just as he had condemned his own partner, because it operates outside the law: 'they're not going to bring him in, they're going to kill him'. The refusal of revenge and the upholding of justice define O'Meara as the moral centre of the film. This dedication initially costs him his partner, then fails to save his adoptive son. 'I've come to bring you in son … the killing's got to stop', he tells Frankie/Rory, who replies, 'Then you're going to have to kill to stop it. Get's a bit complicated, doesn't it?' This final confrontation both invokes and negates the father-son dynamic between the two. It also epitomises the trajectory of homoeroticism in the action thriller. The men achieve physical intimacy through violence: their final embrace occurs when they have shot each other. Frankie/Rory's dying explanation of the failure of good intentions throughout the film is that this is 'not an American story, it's an Irish one'. This is hard to uphold for the film as a whole. Perhaps, however, *The Devil's Own*'s failure as a commercial thriller may derive from its reflection of the complexity of relationships between US security and its others in the film's central 'buddies'.

Ireland, the United States and the world

These films possess a confidence that history is something horrible that happens elsewhere, which is almost eerie in the aftermath of September 11th. The action thriller at the end of the twentieth century echoed the narrative paradigms identified by Stephen Arata in relation to popular adventure fiction at the end of the nineteenth century. Ford in *Patriot Games* is another 'occidental tourist' and, even if the British Isles are not so far east as the exotic destinations of Kipling and H. Rider Haggard, the same pattern of exposure and contamination occurs and the horrible other follows him home. US security, with all the gamut of meaning the phrase implies, is haunted by the shadows of political conflicts that threaten to catch it in nets of political and social consequence beyond its control. These horrible others, like Stoker's Dracula or the conspirators in Conan Doyle's *The Sign of the Four*, are dangerous precisely because they can blend so easily into the anonymity of modern urban environments that are defined by migration, movement, and chance. There is a marked shift from *Patriot Games* to *The Devil's Own*. In the former, danger comes from the unseen stalker on the highway and in the street. In the latter, it comes from the refugee you have invited into your home precisely because he is just like you. The hero in the first instance can ultimately recover his family from tragedy, re-establishing the boundaries between them and us, safety and danger, home and abroad. In *The Devil's Own*, he can neither recuperate the former terrorist into a good American son, as he wishes to do, nor return so easily to a bounded identity. 'If I was 8 years old and saw my father gunned down in front of my family, I'd be carrying a gun too. And I wouldn't be wearing a badge', O'Meara claims. *The Devil's Own* ruptures its own narrative boundaries. O'Meara has become alienated from the police, disregarding orders to co-operate with an implausibly combined FBI and SAS operation which he is convinced aims to kill Frankie/Rory, not arrest him. He is equally alienated from the leading figures in the Irish community, who are complicit in Frankie's gunrunning. There is no stereotype quite so indicative of American political morality as that of the one good cop. O'Meara's form of alienation is typical of the end of conspiracy thrillers, a genre which the director of *The Devil's Own*, Alan J. Pakula, did much to define. *The Devil's Own*, however, does not take the radical chances which made his earlier films like *The Parallax View* (1974) and *Klute* (1971) genre-defining. Faced with the FBI's hostility, O'Meara has the Constitution to protect him: 'Next time you want to talk to me, read me my rights.'

The final scene where O'Meara grieves for the man he has regarded as a son, killed, and tried to save, mirrors the opening scene where Pitt's character is seen with his father prior to the latter's sectarian murder. Both scenes are connected with the sea, and the two men fighting on the boat are sharing the same kind of space as the father and son had shared in the idyllic pre-credit fishing scene. The metaphoric construction of the US as father is hard to miss in these films, even if the special relationship it has with Britain in *Patriot Games* is that of a responsible son caring for a parent country in its dotage. (The stereotypes of English characters in both films, as either quaintly ineffectual or despotically ruthless, are in many ways more offensive than the Irish ones, despite their very different views of the Troubles.)

The action movies of the '90s contain within them maps of imagined global relations defined by two opposed chronotopes, the United States and Ireland, that is, home and abroad. Each of these is in turn defined by a series of internal antinomies of urban and suburban, violent ghetto and rural idyll, familial and public spaces. The cinematic construction of these opposing places maps the imaginary relation between the United States and its (self-) images. The specific role of the Irish Troubles, in this context, is connected to the instability of the boundary between 'them' and 'us' in the '90s. In *The Siege* (Zwick, 1998), which focused on Arab terrorism, the confrontation with an apparently racially identifiable enemy provokes a confrontation between two very different versions of the United States: one epitomised by Denzel Washington as its democratic, individualist, and free-speaking sense of itself as defender of truth and justice; the other played by Bruce Willis as a kind of sub-Macarthur, with a strutting, patriotic sense of US importance. In *The Devil's Own* and *Patriot Games*, the Irish enemy confronted is more like the real terrorist threat that the United States could not admit to itself in the '90s: white, hard to distinguish, related.

In her fascinating study of the Irish-American twenties star Colleen Moore, Diane Negra makes the point that the Irish at that time were the model minority, assimilable advertisements for the immigrant American dream:

> If Irishness connotes transformative potential, such an association carries within it a fundamental dismissal of the desirability of retaining Irish characteristics … Irishness is assimilable in large part due to the fact that it is capable of becoming something else. (45)

In the Hollywood action thrillers of the '90s it seems it was harder to lose the Irish story in a new American one, but Irishness began to connote transformative potential of a different kind. In 1996, just when *The Devil's Own* must have looked like a sure-fire box office hit in production meetings, Bill Clinton made two speeches which featured Northern Ireland prominently. In an address to the Democratic National Convention on 30 August, President Clinton declared that he sought 'to build a bridge to the twenty-first century with the world's strongest defence and a foreign policy that advocates the values of our American community in the community of nations'. In this context he surveyed the US role as arbitrator of international political conflict:

> We have helped to bring democracy to Haiti and peace to Bosnia. Now the peace signed on the White House lawn between the Israelis and the Palestinians must embrace more of Israel's neighbours. The deep desire for peace which Hilary and I felt when we walked the streets of Belfast and Derry must become real for all the people of Northern Ireland. And Cuba must finally join the community of nations. ('Address')

Clinton's address to the United Nations on 24 September of the same year reinforced the parallels, again featuring Bosnia and Haiti briefly before linking developments in Northern Ireland and the Middle East even more explicitly:

> In the Middle East and in Northern Ireland, there is progress towards lasting peace, and we are moving in the right direction. Now we must support continued progress between Israel and Palestinians, and we must broaden the circle of peace to include more of Israel's neighbours. We must help to give the children of Belfast a chance to live out normal lives. ('Remarks')

The imperative case is differently directed here, this time stressing the obligations on the United States rather than the participants in the conflict. Presenting himself to his own party Clinton constructs the United States as in a position to dictate terms to others: addressing the UN, he presents the United States as part of an international community subject to the moral imperative of peacemaking. The contradictions between these two positions have exploded since the change of administration in the United States.

If Ireland had a metonymic relation to terrorism at the beginning of the '90s, by 1996, it had apparently acquired an allegorical function. This new configuration established itself in the thriller genre with the box office success of *The Jackal* (Caton-Jones, 1997). The casting of Richard Gere as the former IRA man indicates the possibility of moral ambiguity, but by the end he has been so far assimilated as to achieve a form of partnership with the FBI man, played with his customary moral authority by Sidney Poitier. The landscape of global politics is now so unstable that it will prove increasingly perplexing for the thriller genre to map. It is impossible to predict how Irish characters and situations will be deployed in the genre in the future, but probable that they will remain as deeply implicated in the discourses of race and gender and as unconcerned with getting the accent right. It is certain, however, that Hollywood will continue to project its hopes and fears onto the troubles of others.

WORKS CITED

Arata, Stephen D. 'The Occidental Tourist: *Dracula* and the anxiety of reverse colonisation'. *Victorian Studies* 33:4 (Summer 1990): 621–45. Rpt. in *The Critical Response to Bram Stoker*, ed. Carol Senf (Westport: Greenwood, 1994); in *Dracula*, ed. Nina Auerbach and David Skal (New York: Norton, 1997); and in *Dracula: A Casebook*, ed. Glennis Byron (London: Macmillan, 1998).

Bakhtin, M.M. *The Dialogical Imagination.* Trans. Caryl Emerson and Michael Holquist. Ed. Michael Holquist. Austin: University of Texas Press, 1981.

Caffrey, David, dir. *Divorcing Jack.* BBC/Winchester/Scala, 1998.

Caton-Jones, Michael, dir. *The Jackal.* Universal/Mutual/Alphaville, 1997.

Clinton, William. 'Clinton Address to Democratic National Convention'. United Center, Chicago. 29 Aug. 1996. <usinfo.state.gov/journals/itps/1096/ijpe/clin1.htm>.

—. 'Remarks by President Clinton in Address to the 51st General Assembly of the United Nations'. United Nations, New York. 24 Sept. 1996. <http://www.jfklibrary.org/clinton_un_address.html>.

Cohan, Steven, and Ina Rae Hark, eds. *Screening the Male: Exploring Masculinities in Hollywood Cinema.* London and New York: Routledge, 1993.

Donner, Richard, dir. *Lethal Weapon.* Warner Brothers, 1987.

Fuchs, Cynthia. 'The Buddy Politic'. Cohan and Hark 194–213.

Giles, Jeff. 'Cool. Excellent. Thanks'. Interview with Brad Pitt. *Newsweek,* 3 February 1997: 50.

McLoone, Martin. *Irish Film: The Emergence of a Contemporary Cinema.* London: BFI, 2000.

Massood, Paula J. 'City Spaces and City Times: Bakhtin's Chronotope and Recent African-American Film'. *Screening the City.* Ed. Mark Shiel and Tony Fitzmaurice. London and New York: Verso, 2003. 200–15.

Mulvey, Laura. 'Visual Pleasure and Narrative Cinema'. *Screen* 16.3 (1975): 6–18.

—. 'Afterthoughts on "Visual Pleasure and Narrative Cinema" Inspired by King Vidor's *Duel in the Sun*'. *Framework* 15–17 (1981): 12–15.

Neale, Steve. 'Masculinity as Spectacle'. *Screen* 24.6 (1983). Rpt. in Cohan and Hark 9–20.

Negra, Diane. *Off-White Hollywood: American Culture and Ethnic Female Stardom.* London and New York: Routledge, 2001.

Noyce, Phillip, dir. *Patriot Games.* UIP/Paramount, 1992.

Pakula, Alan J., dir. *The Devil's Own.* Columbia, 1997.

—. *The Parallax View.* Paramount/Gus/Harbour/Doubleday, 1974.

—. *Klute.* Warner Brothers, 1971.

Pellingham, Mark, dir. *Arlington Road.* Sony/Screen Gems/Lakeshore Entertainment, 1999.

Sedgwick, Eve Kosofsky. *Between Men: English Literature and Male Homosocial Desire.* New York: Columbia UP, 1985.

Sobchack, Vivian. 'Lounge Time: Postwar Crises and the Chronotope of *Film Noir*'. *Refiguring American Film Genres: Theory and History.* Ed. Nick Browne. Berkeley: University of California Press, 1998. 129–70.

Tasker, Yvonne. *Spectacular Bodies: Gender, Genre and the Action Cinema.* London and New York: Routledge, 1993.

Zwick, Edward, dir. *The Siege.* 20th Century Fox, 1998.

The Northern other: Southern Irish cinema and the Troubles

DES O'RAWE

> My job is making films, finding new forms for a new content.
> *Tout va bien* (Godard and Gorin, 1972)

The history of the cinema is filled with examples of radical filmmaking practices and positions that emerged in times and places of acute instability and conflict. In their respective cultures, for example, films by Eisenstein, Vertov, Buñuel, Renoir, Visconti, Pontecorvo, and Godard continue to provoke reflection on the role of the cinema and its ability to inform and transform perceptions of civil society and the nature of power-relations. *Strike* (1925), *Man with a Movie Camera* (1929), *Land without Bread* (1933), *La Vie est à nous* (1936), *La Terra Trema* (1948), *The Battle of Algiers* (1965), and *Tout va bien* (1972) still resonate with the promise that dangerous times can generate dissident forms, and still suggest that in every new society there is always the possibility of a new cinema. Indeed, the testimony of these films is that, contrary to popular belief, a political cinema is not necessarily a cinema of direct politicization anymore than it is a cinema that devotes itself solely to the fictional or documentary representation of specific political incidents and ideas. Rather, it relates to a more elusive phenomenon: a cinematic experience that is intimately connected to the actualities and contradictions of fundamental political and cultural moments. To borrow Godard's important distinction: a political film is not *about* politics; it *is* politics.

Throughout the Troubles, the cinema largely failed to produce anything resembling a genuinely political contribution to the issues and events that shaped Northern Irish society. In general, feature-length 'Troubles films' were afflicted by diffident realism, generic conventionality and – at their worst – a naïve assumption that such films might make something happen. These shortcomings might at least be understandable if they applied solely to mainstream Euro-American productions where political irrelevance is regarded as a virtue. However, Irish filmmakers themselves proved especially incapable of finding the resources necessary to offer an aesthetically meaningful and politically intelligent alternative to this trend. This essay will attempt to address the causes and implications of this particular phenomenon. What was it precisely that stifled the flowering of a radical and inventive indigenous cinema in Ireland, one that could have counted amongst its achievements the creation of new ways of visualising and engaging with the Troubles? Why was Irish cinema so unable (or unwilling) to offer filmic forms and situations that could subvert the representational regimes of its more mainstream counterparts and sponsors? How does one explain the contradiction between the conventional formal and narrative strategies employed by Irish filmmakers and the disruptive, fragmenting, and very dangerous political situations that appeared to have provoked films such as *Cal* (O'Connor, 1984), *In the Name of the Father* (Sheridan, 1993), and *Nothing Personal* (O'Sullivan, 1995)? Perhaps instead of asking 'How has Irish cinema represented the Troubles?' we should ask 'What challenges has the Troubles represented for Irish cinema?'

Hill and after

The *locus classicus* of academic discussions about the representation of the Troubles in mainstream American, British, and Irish cinema is John Hill's 'Images of Violence' chapter in *Cinema and Ireland*. Published in 1987, Hill's thesis has remained an indispensable reference point for all subsequent contributions to this debate, contributions that have – by and large – dutifully augmented and updated Hill's analysis on its own terms. Notwithstanding subtle changes of emphasis and shifts in intellectual perspective, the materialist assumptions enunciated by Hill have never been fundamentally challenged. In essence, Hill contrasts the narrative and expressive function of violence within Hollywood, where it 'resolves all problems and tensions', with what he considers to be the traditional image of violence in British cinema, where it 'characteristically thwarts drives and ambitions, indicates character flaw or lack of self-identity, exacerbates problems and tensions and signifies either regression or fatalism' (Rockett, Gibbons, and Hill, 151–2). (From a materialist perspective, such differences are largely incidental: Hollywood and British cinema's versions of the Troubles have traditionally configured the causes and conditions of Irish political violence in terms of racial madness and residual metaphysics.) After discussing the distortion and expurgation of 'history' from a selection of Hollywood and British treatments of Ireland, Hill rounds on two Irish films of the 1980s, *Angel* (Jordan, 1982) and *Cal*, and laments that 'many of the same attitudes and assumptions' that characterised external cinematic representations of the Troubles 'are now appearing in the work of Irish film makers' (Rockett, Gibbons, and Hill, 178). For Hill, *Angel* and *Cal* were less examples of an emergent Irish political cinema than further instances of someone else's wine in an Irish bottle: 'As with so many British films before them, *Angel* and *Cal* have proved unequal to the challenge of their subject matter and, as a result, have obscured, as much as they have illuminated, the issues with which they have dealt' (Rockett, Gibbons, and Hill, 184).

In the years that followed the publication of *Cinema and Ireland*, Irish film criticism has diligently followed the trail blazed by (Irish) cultural studies, insofar as it has proffered a critical practice that promotes an understanding of film-meaning in terms of stereotype analysis, historicism (new and old), and occasional speculations derived from post-colonial and 'Third Cinema' theory.[1] Admittedly, the general complaint – that 'Troubles films' invariably omit and mystify the material causes and conditions of the conflict – has been augmented by further and more specific accusations. It has been argued, for example, that such films, in relying on a prescribed range of generic models (principally, melodrama and the thriller), have also reproduced the phallocentric bias (and basis) of Northern Irish political culture.[2] Increasingly, the criticism that such films consistently – even religiously – misrepresent the Protestant-unionist experience has also been articulated with greater confidence. In the 1990s, for example, Brian McIlroy introduced historical revisionism into Irish Film Studies. He argued that the majority of Irish and Irish-related films marginalized and caricatured the Protestant and unionist position: 'visual representations [of the Troubles] have assisted in the building of Catholic nationalist and republican self-esteem at the expense of the link to actual historical and present realities' (*Shooting to Kill*, 200). Although McIlroy also addressed some of the representational deficiencies and anomalies that have accompanied filmic depictions of women's experiences and struggles within this context, his over-riding concern has been to identify and redress what he considers to be the endemic 'nativism' and 'anti-unionism' that thrives within external and indigenous cinematic and televisual representations of the Troubles.[3]

Although such interventions have assisted in identifying other arenas of 'misrepresentation', they have done so by intensifying – rather than challenging – prevailing critical orthodoxies about the significance of historical inaccuracy and the consequences of genre restraint in Irish cinema. This approach to the issue of filmic representation, and to the representation of the Troubles in particular, remains predicated on the assumption that any comparative analysis of Irish cinema is only valid if the comparison relates to the (mainstream) cinemas of America and Britain. This paradigm has surely served its purpose and must now be replaced by approaches that

---

1 McLoone discusses Ireland and the Third Cinema question in *Irish Film*, 122–8. See also Willemen, 'Third Cinema', 1–29 and Wayne. 2 See Edge, 211–17 and Farley, 203–14. 3 See also Pettitt, *Screening Ireland*, 258–64.

situate contemporary Irish cinema within a much wider creative, industrial, and critical context. Arguably, the condition of Irish cinema and of Irish film criticism can
be analysed very productively when set against the experiences and achievements of
non-European, non-American contemporary filmmakers (Amos Gitai, for example)
who have worked against 'Hollywood' rather than with it, and who have involved
themselves in a creative and critical project that fundamentally re-orientates the relationship between cinematic discourses and cultural practices.[4] Such comparisons
unflatteringly reveal certain deficiencies of Irish cinema, but they also compel us to
investigate more thoroughly the reasons why genuinely 'new' forms have been so rare
in Irish cinema, and virtually non-existent in films that seek to explore the political
complexities of the Troubles.

Pragmatism and a politique

While various rationales have occasionally been proffered in defence of the representational gaps and contingencies that have afflicted Irish 'Troubles films', such positions tend to congratulate compromise rather than to demand greater institutional
defiance and artistic integrity. In her recent study of Jim Sheridan's films, Ruth Barton
argues that *In the Name of the Father*, for all its shortcomings as a serious political
film, should be appreciated within the context of 'popular cinema'. In this regard, she
suggests, it is a political film to the extent that it successfully injects 'an array of local
concerns into a popular, universal format in a manner that few other contemporary
Irish films have achieved' (98). This argument certainly confronts the problematic
relationship between the popular and the political, but it also privileges a cinema in
search of an external audience over one that is in search of actual engagement. In relation to *The Boxer* (Sheridan, 1997), for example, Barton assesses some of the failings
of this film alongside Thaddeus O'Sullivan's *Nothing Personal* and concludes that:
'The political confusions that mark *The Boxer* and many other films born of the peace
process must be read against a background of popular uncertainty as to the real
potential for institutional and communal accord within Northern Ireland' (122).
Alternatively, what is significant about films such as *The Boxer* and *Nothing Personal*
is less a case of what they reflect than what they continue to project: an allegiance to
narrative and generic conventionality that prevents any meaningful relationship
between a filmic mode of expression and a 'background' of political uncertainty. In
this regard, *The Boxer*'s failure 'to open up a space where the legacy of [the Troubles]

4 On Gitai's work, see Willemen, 'Bangkok', 162–74.

can be represented' in novel and challenging ways is typical of broader developments within 'post-ceasefire' cinema (McLoone, *Irish Film,* 84). Indeed, it is hard to disagree with Martin McLoone's general conclusion that

> the cinema that has so far emerged ... has largely played on the existing tra-
> ditions of representing violence ... In most cases, it is not just that the films
> are decidedly apolitical, more they are studiously anti-political ... In the end,
> this cinema's relationship to the present is that it reminds us of the past and
> so underpins the necessity for continuing the search for peace. That this is the
> extent of its political sophistication is disappointing and only reinforces the
> feeling that cinema in general today ... has lost its ability or its potential for
> radical politics and social analysis. (*Irish Film,* 84)[5]

However, before embarking on a broader analysis of the relationship between Southern Irish cinema and the Troubles it is instructive to consider the recent work of Richard Kirkland. In questioning the continued relevance of existing approaches to cinematic representations of the Troubles, Kirkland refers to an alternative critical tradition that certainly has the potential to offer a more radical analysis of the role of realism, apparatus, and ideology in the formation and reception of (what Kirkland loosely categorises as) 'Northern Irish cinema'. Whilst granting Hill's position some 'seductive coherence not least because it conclusively identifies blame', Kirkland is generally unimpressed by 'Irish materialist film criticism', which he describes as 'an unfeasible project [whose] existence is predicated on the identification of fragments of the [bourgeois] totality, missed opportunities and hopeful aspirations'. Using 'the critical frameworks established by Jean-Louis Comolli, Jean-Pierre Oudart and Jean Narboni in the journal *Cahiers du Cinéma*', Kirkland unearths 'a materialist analysis that can account for recent developments in Northern Irish cinema, [and] take cognisance of Hill's earlier demands, but avoid the utopian circlings implicit in the "what exists/what should exist" opposition' (33–4). In this analysis of 'Northern Irish cinema', Kirkland applies the uncompromising structuralism of 'Comolli/Oudart/ Narboni' to films like *In the Name of the Father, Hidden Agenda* (Loach, 1990), *Angel, Cal,* and *The Long Good Friday* (MacKenzie, 1979). Only Margo Harkin's *Hush-a-*

---

5 McLoone's chagrin has no doubt been aggravated by the fact that many 'younger' Southern Irish filmmakers – for example, Fintan Connolly, Martin Duffy, and Gerry Stembridge – increasingly appear to regard a cinema appropriate to a new, economically transformed and progressive Ireland as being one that offers its audiences flashy essays on yesterday's tyrants, today's middle-class angst, and visitors from outer space. In the work of someone like Trish McAdam, in particular, we are being offered a 'lifestyle' cinema that seems to pander to the 'lifestyle' preoccupations of an ideologically inert society.

Bye Baby (1989) survives the onslaught unscathed. For Kirkland, *Hush-a-Bye Baby* remains an exemplary (British-funded) Irish political film largely because it refuses to offer a transcendent and genre-determined resolution to the political contradictions that it represents. Unlike *The Crying Game* (Jordan, 1992) – which Kirkland does not entirely dismiss – *Hush-a-Bye Baby* 'maintains the creative tensions of the various cultural oppositions that afflict [its protagonist] and in acknowledging their symbiotic nature, the film forbids the possibility of such formations proving redemptive' (70).⁶

The 'Comolli/Oudart/Narboni' framework offers the possibility of a critical approach to 'Northern Irish cinema' that replaces the fixation on the representation of 'stereotypical characters and situations' with a much-needed emphasis on 'the transparency of the ideology of identitarianism as the natural, preordained area of enquiry and dilemma' (Kirkland, 36). However, situating 'Northern Irish cinema' and 'Irish materialist film criticism' within the context of *Cahiers du Cinéma* (c.1969–72) also highlights, all too obviously, the fact that Irish cinema (unlike French cinema) has always struggled to construct an indigenous history and has failed to sustain a critical practice capable of responding to that history. The crisis within contemporary Irish film criticism is the product of the crisis that is Irish cinema. (To anyone unexcited by the prospect of an *ad infinitum* analysis of the representation of politics and the politics of representation, Irish cinema remains an unattractive object of study.) While Kirkland does not entirely disagree with this assessment, he does adopt a particularly deterministic paradigm whose application to 'Northern Irish cinema' is never entirely plausible. Inevitably, the application of this *politique* is problematic in relation both to the (necessarily) narrow range of films Kirkland discusses and within a wider (comparative) context that must, first and foremost, acknowledge the specific ideological motivations behind *Cahiers du Cinéma's* radical change of intellectual direction in the 1960s.⁷

If the strategies of this *Cahiers* project are relevant to the study of 'Northern Irish cinema', it is, arguably, *vis-à-vis* the politics of film production in Northern Ireland itself, rather than to a materialist critique of filmic representations of Northern Ireland

---

6 Following Brian Neve, Kirkland believes that 'during the 1990s, a distinct historical turn can be recognized in cinematic representations of the North to a degree so startling that it is hard not to see the overall tendency as a mode of redress' (33). This 'overall tendency', he suggests, has been characterized by both 'a greater degree of formal sophistication' and a new willingness to recognise and analyse the complexities of Northern Irish cultural identity. Slightly modified narrative structures and an eagerness to embrace 'identity' contradictions in films about Northern Ireland are arguably less 'startling' when viewed in relation to broader shifts of tone and emphasis within recent British and European cinema. See Neve, 2–8.   7 Browne provides an over-view of these issues in relation to *Cahiers du Cinéma* and French film culture (1–7). Atack is also well worth consulting.

and the Troubles. Admittedly, this type of distinction is never easy to sustain but it does afford us a moment to reflect upon the institutional and cultural forces that appear to have stifled the emergence of a political cinema within Northern Ireland itself. To what extent, for example, have the fraught politics of Northern Ireland determined the granting and withholding of financial support for film production? What kinds of film do the Arts Council of Northern Ireland, the Northern Ireland Film and Television Commission, the 'conflict resolution' industry and the BBC want made? What are the ('structural') relations between these institutions, and what are the real implications of the tension between cultural management and artistic responsibility for Northern Irish cinema? Arguably, Northern Irish filmmakers in particular have been compromised by a political situation that has enabled such organizations to emerge as visionary sponsors of a (post-Troubles) Northern Ireland where the rhetoric of 'political inclusion' and neo-liberal optimism is assumed to be a natural alternative to real political disagreement. This situation, allied to the perpetually embryonic condition of indigenous cinema in the South, has certainly militated against the emergence of a tradition of filmmaking in Ireland that is truly political in form and content. Furthermore, in considering the relationship between Southern Irish cinema and the Troubles, one must also attend to an added factor that has enjoyed little real visibility within contemporary Irish film criticism: when it comes to dealing with the North, Southern Irish cinema has itself been a peculiarly fearful cultural enterprise.

A fearful cinema

From a Northern perspective, it is difficult not to become intrigued by the ways in which Southern Irish cinema has constructed the Troubles, and the motivations behind that construction. Whilst directors like Jordan and O'Sullivan have always been willing to move beyond a mainstream realist aesthetic, as has Sheridan in some of his theatre projects, their cinematic representations of the Troubles have remained remarkably faithful to the stereotypical 'confusions' and historically specific connotations that have traditionally been a feature of mainstream cinema. Even the associations seem to be disassociative. Consider, for example, the sight of Ian McIlhenny boasting about 'a bit of Belfast efficiency' before being blown to smithereens in *Michael Collins* (Jordan, 1996), or the daft spectacle of the *Riverdance*-inspired sequence at the beginning of *Some Mother's Son* (George, 1996), or the pretentious tribute to *The Battle of Algiers* at the end of *Nothing Personal*. All of these are hardly instances of imaginative engage-

ment with the complexities of the Troubles. Rather they are examples of a displacement strategy that has been all too common in Southern Irish films *about* Northern
Irish politics. Inevitably, narrative films – whether shaped around an antagonism
between a 'good' (reformed/responsible/realistic) terrorist-hero and a 'bad' (psychotic/
anarchic/insane) terrorist-villain, around Oedipal trajectories, and/or a 'love across the
barricades' trope – are not normally conducive to the production of politically intelligent cinema. While Hill and others had predicted this phenomenon as far back as
the 1980s, it has become increasingly difficult to accept explanations of this predispo-
sition that are founded almost entirely on the acknowledged necessity of popularity
and the vicissitudes of industry: the templates and clichés that have been adopted and
adapted by contemporary Irish cinema in its encounters with the Troubles cannot be
explained simply in terms of distribution opportunities and the tyrannies of the box-
office. It was not simply that the Troubles were an *event* to be fictionalized in accordance with the reactionary logic and commercial rationale of popular cinema, but that
such cinematic tendencies served to further immunise the 'progressive' South from the
'primitive' North.[8] Sheridan would no doubt feel some justification in rejecting this
argument: did not *In the Name of the Father, Some Mother's Son,* and *The Boxer* engage,
inform, and generate debate about the Troubles, the activities of the British state, and
the morality of republican violence? While this is true to some extent, it is also true
that the content of these films significantly 'post-dated' their immediate political relevance. It should be remembered that Sheridan and George's 'Troubles Trilogy' dealt
with (and in) issues that already had settled interpretations within the discursive economy of Northern Irish politics. Perhaps Sheridan's 'political vision' merely amounts to
a belief that there is a place for sentimentality and opportunism within political
cinema, but, if nothing else, the international debates about political cinema from the
1960s and 1970s have taught us that such a vision is usually fraudulent and always
counter-productive.

Similar contradictions and inconsistencies can be identified in the work of
Thaddeus O'Sullivan and Neil Jordan. *December Bride* (O'Sullivan, 1990), for example, declares an association (that is both visual and contextual) with Northern Irish
Protestant-unionist history. Yet, from the perspective of 1990 (when the film was first
released) there is something suspiciously savoury about this relationship: O'Sullivan's
adaptational priorities and aesthetic scheme use the past to displace the present.[9] In
its focus on the 'Protestant family', and on arenas of schism and dissent within that

---

8 For a discussion of constitutional and attitudinal issues relating to the Republic of Ireland's 'construction' of
the North that includes a particularly trenchant analysis of *The Crying Game*, see Cleary, 97–141.   9 For an
alternative view of *December Bride*, see Pettitt, *December Bride* and McLoone, '*December Bride*'.

'family', *December Bride* deftly steers clear of the defining political issue in Northern Irish history and politics, namely, the conflict between Protestants and Catholics. In adapting Bell's novel, O'Sullivan and David Rudkin sought to give the Northern Protestant (Presbyterian) community a pastoral radiance and societal complexity that had hitherto seemed the preserve of an imagined Catholic-nationalist experience. A key feature of this strategy involved softening the characterisation of Sarah Gomartin (Saskia Reeves) and finessing the novel's obdurate realism and emphasis on sectarian animosity. The epic scope and pastoral radiance of O'Sullivan's *mise-en-scène* contradicts both Bell's bleak vision of Northern Ireland and his novel's uncompromising portrayal of the local hatreds that have governed that war-torn region. Ultimately, the cinematic adaptation of *December Bride* confirms that it is more difficult to landscape the people accurately than it is to people the landscape differently. A similar displacement strategy is discernible in *Nothing Personal*, a film that seems to pride itself on being as much about anywhere as it is about Belfast in the 1970s. Anywhere is too close to nowhere, and although the 'content' of the film evokes a certain time, place, and moral mentality, its forms do not. *Nothing Personal* reproduces 'images of violence' that dutifully conform to the stylistic and narrative models of contemporary (Hollywood/ British) gangster films. While his skilful appropriation of such conventions may be regarded as a praiseworthy achievement in some quarters, O'Sullivan's strategy has really no allegiance to a cinema that seeks to subvert standardized filmic tropes and structures in order to transform perceptions of historical and political realities.

The tangential engagement with the Troubles in some of Neil Jordan's work likewise seems to betray not just an unavoidable distortion of the 'facts', but a tendency to delimit the relevance of the Troubles to the political values and preoccupations of contemporary southern Irish society. Richard Kearney and John Hill have famously disagreed about the representation of violence in *Angel*,[10] for example, and yet watching this film, over twenty years after it was first released, one is struck not so much by *Angel*'s aesthetic ambitions (or metaphysical complexity) but by the degree to which it studiously says nothing that might be construed as being immediately relevant to political developments in Northern Ireland in the early 1980s. Indeed, the expressionistic adumbration of the Troubles in *Angel* now seems oddly typical of Southern Irish cinema's ambivalent attitude towards Northern Ireland. The case of *Michael Collins* is more complicated, not least because of its generic orientations and distribution history. It should be noted that *Michael Collins* is – primarily – an historical epic, and therefore, like all historical epics, the product of a 'post-historical'

10 See Rockett, Gibbons, and Hill, 178–81 and Kearney, 175–83.

perception. While the film provoked controversy (albeit almost exclusively in relation to its dramatisation of historical events and personalities) it also conveyed a
strong sense of the North – and *its* Troubles – as being absent from the 'end of history' festivities held in the South throughout the 1990s. Indeed, the film's homage to
those seeking to 'take the gun out of Irish politics' can too readily seem a patronising
pat on the back rather than a genuine expression of shared responsibility.[11] Ultimately,
films like *Angel, The Crying Game*, and *Michael Collins* only represent the Troubles
for metaphorical effect: they invoke a side-show that distracts their audience from
serious reflection on the presence of Republican violence within the political subconscious of Jordan's own society.

The only time at which this fear of the North might have been confronted was
during the 1970s and 1980s, a period when Ireland did produce a number of formally
inventive and politically intelligent films. And yet, even here the Troubles were generally less important than the Church, the family, the changing role of women, and
myths of nation. If *Maeve* (Murphy and Davies, 1991) and *Hush-a-Bye Baby* are still
amongst the most important films from this period, it is because they are (Northern
Irish) films that seem more alert to the idea that political and social issues in the South
are inextricably linked to political developments in the North. Similarly, despite the
undeniable importance of films directed by Cathal Black, Bob Quinn, and Kieran
Hickey during this period, only Joe Comerford's *Reefer and the Model* (1988), *High
Boot Benny* (1993), and, to some extent, *Traveller* (1981)[12] constitute some recognition
of the complexities of the Troubles. However, such films invariably negotiate this
problem by foregrounding the border as a crucial site of cultural definition and political significance.[13] It might be suggested that, had the 'new' Irish cinema movement
of the 1970s and 1980s developed into something culturally substantial and artisti-
cally exceptional, Comerford's 'incursions' would have prepared the way for other
Southern filmmakers to explore the paradoxes of partition through the deployment
of increasingly experimental and formally disruptive strategies. This I doubt: an Irish
political cinema has rendered itself unfeasible because it has been afraid of infection
from the virus of Northern political violence. While this fear was understandable and
possibly even natural, its implications for the development of new ways of repre-

11 For a useful discussion of critical reactions to *Michael Collins*, see Rockett and Rockett, 163–77. See also
McIlroy's discussion of *Michael Collins*, in which he concludes that 'Jordan's film reaffirms the anti-imperialist
myth … that republicans need deal only with Britain and not with the Ulster protestants and the Unionist
voter, who are judged as weak and "deluded lackeys". For the Unionist audience, then, Jordan's *Michael Collins*
crosses the border and visualises them out of history' (28).   12 See Hooper, 179–91.   13 O'Sullivan's *In the
Border Country* is clearly also relevant within this context. For some comment on this sub-genre, see Haslam,
136, 144n19.

senting, interrogating, and relating to the Troubles have been more debilitating than has been generally recognized.

Conclusion

Clearly, in attempting to answer the question 'What did the Troubles represent for Irish cinema?' one would have to accept that a genuinely political cinema can only emerge in places where an established, organically productive, and intellectually vibrant film culture already exists. This is the only kind of cinema that would be capable of, and willing to, create image formations and filmic situations that could confront and transcend the traumatic politics and tragic paradoxes of the Troubles. The examples of political cinema cited at the beginning of this essay share one important historical factor: they emerged in societies that already possessed an established film culture and tradition of formal experimentation that allowed their filmmakers to refer to a 'history' that would underwrite the relevance of the cinema to contemporary politics. Such films exist both within a past that has harnessed and reconfigured emergent political realities and within a present, as in the very obvious in the case of a film like *Tout va bien*, that is able to reflect upon what may or may not be possible in the after-life of a political moment, that is, the defeat of radical ideals and their absorption into mainstream political culture. If 'Irish materialist film criticism' has been a discourse doomed to continually ponder 'absence' and ruminate on its own deficiencies, it has also rarely sought to find a way out of this *via negativa* through the wider history of cinema and through an encounter with the possibility that the cinema is sometimes more political than politics. For this reason, it should be imperative that Irish film criticism begins the urgent work of exploring, within a more vigorously comparative context, positions and practices that will encourage the next generation of Irish filmmakers to 'find new forms for new contents'. Reinterpreting the South's relationship with Northern Ireland, and confronting the differences, paradoxes, and fears that define that relationship, will be crucial to this process. The prospects for an Irish political cinema are not limited solely by the terminally fragile nature of the Irish film industry's indigenous means of production and distribution, any more than they are assisted by a critical practice that remains preoccupied with the vagaries of cultural representation. While these industrial and institutional factors have certainly served to inhibit and circumscribe the emergence of a meaningful political cinema in Ireland, they have not been the only cause of its failure. Fear has also been a factor – the fear of a film that *is* politics.

WORKS CITED

Atack, Margaret. *May 68 in French Fiction and Film: Rethinking Society, Rethinking Representation.* Oxford: Oxford UP, 1999.

Barton, Ruth. *Jim Sheridan: Framing the Nation.* Dublin: Liffey Press, 2002.

Browne, Nick, ed. *Cahiers du Cinéma: 1969–1972: The Politics of Representation.* Cambridge, Mass.: Harvard UP, 1990.

Buñuel, Luis, dir. *Land Without Bread / Las Hurdes.* Spain, 1933.

Cleary, Joe. *Literature, Partition and the Nation-State: Culture and Conflict in Ireland, Israel and Palestine.* Cambridge: Cambridge UP, 2002.

Comerford, Joe, dir. *High Boot Benny.* Ireland, 1993.

—, dir. *Reefer and the Model.* Ireland, 1988.

—, dir. *Traveller.* Ireland, 1981.

Edge, Sarah. 'Representing Gender and National Identity'. *Rethinking Northern Ireland.* Ed. David Miller. Harlow: Longman, 1998. 211–17.

Eisenstein, Sergei, dir. *Strike / Stachka.* USSR, 1925.

Farley, Fidelma. 'In the Name of the Family: Masculinity and Fatherhood in Contemporary Northern Irish Films'. *Irish Studies Review.* 9.2 (2001): 203–14.

George, Terry, dir. *Some Mother's Son.* Ireland, 1996.

Godard, Jean-Luc, and Jean-Pierre Gorin, dir. *Tout va bien / All's Well.* France, 1972.

Harkin, Margo, dir. *Hush-a-Bye Baby.* Ireland / UK, 1989.

Haslam, Richard. 'Irish Film: Screening the Republic'. *Writing the Irish Republic: Literature, Culture, Politics: 1949–1999.* Ed. Ray Ryan. Basingstoke: Macmillan, 2000. 130–46.

Hooper, Keith. 'A Gallous Story and a Dirty Deed: Word and Image in Neil Jordan and Joe Comerford's *Traveller* (1981)'. *Irish Studies Review* 9.2 (2001): 179–91.

Jordan, Neil, dir. *Angel.* Ireland, 1982.

—, dir. *The Crying Game.* UK, 1992.

—, dir. *Michael Collins.* Ireland / UK, 1996.

Kearney, Richard. *Transitions: Narratives in Modern Irish Culture.* Manchester: Manchester UP, 1988.

Kirkland, Richard. *Identity Parades: Northern Irish Culture and Dissident Subjects.* Liverpool: Liverpool UP, 2002.

Loach, Ken, dir. *Hidden Agenda.* UK, 1990.

McIlroy, Brian. 'History Without Borders: Neil Jordan's *Michael Collins*'. MacKillop 22–8.

—. *Shooting to Kill: Filmmaking and the 'Troubles' in Northern Ireland.* 2nd ed. Richmond, B.C.: Steveston Press, 2001.

MacKenzie, John, dir. *The Long Good Friday.* UK, 1979.

MacKillop, James, ed. *Contemporary Irish Cinema: From* The Quiet Man *to* Dancing at Lughnasa. New York: Syracuse UP, 1999.

McLoone, Martin. '*December Bride:* A Landscape Peopled Differently'. MacKillop 40–53.

—. *Irish Film: The Emergence of a Contemporary Cinema.* London: BFI, 2000.

Murphy, Pat, and John Davies, dir. *Maeve.* UK, 1991.

Neve, Brian. 'Cinema, the Ceasefire and "the Troubles"'. *Irish Studies Review* 20 (1997): 2–8.

O'Connor, Pat, dir. *Cal.* UK, 1984.

O'Sullivan, Thaddeus, dir. *December Bride.* Ireland / UK, 1990.

—, dir. *In the Border Country*, UK, 1991.

—, dir. *Nothing Personal*. Ireland / UK, 1995.

Pettitt, Lance. *December Bride*. Cork: Cork UP/IFI, 2001.

—. *Screening Ireland: Film and Television Representation*. Manchester: Manchester UP, 2000.

Pontecorvo, Gillo, dir. *The Battle of Algiers / La Battaglia di Algeri*. Algeria/Italy, 1965.

Renoir, Jean, dir. *La Vie est à nous People of France*. France, 1936.

Rockett, Kevin, Luke Gibbons, and John Hill. *Cinema and Ireland*. New York: Syracuse UP, 1988.

Rockett, Kevin, and Emer Rockett. *Neil Jordan: Exploring Boundaries*. Dublin: Lilliput Press, 2003.

Sheridan, Jim, dir. *The Boxer*. US / Ireland, 1997.

—, dir. *In the Name of the Father*. Ireland / UK / US, 1993.

Vertov, Dziga, dir. *Man With a Movie Camera / Chelovek s Kinoapparatom*. USSR, 1929.

Visconti, Luchino, dir. *La Terra Trema: Episodio del mare/ The Earth Trembles*. Italy, 1948.

Wayne, Mike. *Political Film: The Dialectics of Third Cinema*. London: Pluto, 2001.

Willemen, Paul. 'The Third Cinema Question: Notes and Reflections'. *Questions of Third Cinema*. Ed. Jim Pines and Paul Willemen. London: BFI, 1989. 1–29.

—. 'Bangkok - Bahrain - Berlin - Jerusalem: Amos Gitai's Editing'. *Looks and Frictions: Essays in Cultural Studies and Film Theory*. London: BFI, 1994. 162–74.

Shall we dance? Movement metaphors as political discourse

J'AIME MORRISON

In his opening remarks, 'Representing the Troubles' conference chair Terence Brown challenged participants to consider the 'energies of the street' in our discussions of the Troubles in Northern Ireland. Brown called for scholars to attend to the 'aesthetics of protest' by examining those moments when violence and aesthetics are joined in periods of social unrest. Fiction and non-fiction writers have eloquently addressed the history of the Troubles through historical narrative, autobiography, poetry, and testimonial in an effort to transcribe their experience. Writing the Troubles has been one of the most significant ways to come to terms with the violence that has characterized Northern Ireland's recent history. The emphasis at this conference on various forms of representation encourages an expanded analysis of this history, one that includes photography, visual art, cinema, and dance. These cultural forms serve as alternate modes of historical inscription. They narrate a history of the unspoken by highlighting the stories of the body.

I am particularly interested in how Brown's 'energies of the street' become formalized during social events such as parades, political negotiations, and instances of violent encounter. What is the relationship between movement and mobilization? When does walking become marching? What is the difference between playing a drum and beating a drum, between a procession and a parade? These differences are manifest in techniques of the body that have been learned and performed through generations. The performance of politically motivated movement encodes years of sectarian feeling, territorial struggle, and political conflict within the body. I am concerned here with how the Troubles have been represented, but also with how the body serves as a record of this conflict, as an embodied transcript.

Movements that enact territorial claims, movements that are censored, movements that cross borders, violent movements, and movements of resistance: all of these actions revise the meaning of urban social space by physically inscribing the historical landscape and investing it with agency. Because of its kinetic consciousness, dance provides a unique perspective to assess the means through which social movements are realised. As dance scholar Randy Martin suggests, 'the very manner in which bodies gather is as important to consider as the ideological or intellectual pursuits that inspired them' (*Critical Moves,* 12). Martin urges us to 'imagine politics from within mobilization, instead of considering power as an external force that seeks to move people' (*Critical Moves,* 12). In short, the physical and the political are engaged in moments of dynamic social choreography, and there is power in these movements.

This study initially considers how dance has been invoked cinematically in relation to the Troubles, and moves toward an analysis of how the vocabulary of dance - specifically, choreography - has been subsumed into Northern Ireland's political lexicon. This choreographic vocabulary calls for an increased attention to the political, social, and cultural contexts in which all movements are performed. Referring to sketches and photographs, as well as to accounts by political analysts, commentators, and politicians, I detail how dance has been invoked in film, on paper, and in practice during the conflict and the negotiations of the late 1990s, which led to the Good Friday/Belfast Agreement of 1998. In what follows I trace the crucial impact of political choreography on these negotiations in order to examine the individual and social movements that have shaped Northern Ireland's political landscape in recent years.

Some Mother's Son (1996), co-written by Terry George and Jim Sheridan, dramatizes the events that led up to the 1981 Hunger Strikes initiated in protest of the treatment of IRA prisoners. The film portrays the relationship between the mothers of two imprisoned hunger strikers and their respective moral dilemmas over whether or not to force their sons off the strike. The film also draws attention to wider territorial disputes between the nationalist community and the British government during the 1960s and '70s. Throughout the film, various forms of movement come under surveillance and are subject to control, including dance.

British soldiers block Annie, one of the mothers, as she tries to herd her cattle down a road that has been marked 'unapproved'. This scene illustrates the government's plan to isolate the more radical Republican communities of the North by monitoring their travel on roads and closing the border, and references the British military's campaign to blow up bridges and tunnels to hinder the possibility of illegal arms transportation. 'They want to control us!' says a member of the IRA. Later in the film the other mother, Kathleen, is detained at a routine checkpoint while driving to work. Such constraints are depicted as being at the heart of the British campaign to immobilize the IRA and the nationalist community. These two initial scenes of confrontation draw attention to the strategic importance of restricting the physical mobility of Catholics during the Troubles.

In the most striking scene of the film, the movements of Irish step dance are juxtaposed with the choreography of an IRA ambush. The blood-pumping rhythms of

Irish music sound out a battle call over the soundtrack as members of an IRA unit make their way to an ambush target, planned in retaliation for the destruction of a bridge. Inter-cut with this scene are images of young female Irish step dancers who beat out their own anxious rhythms as the camera moves back and forth between shots of dancers' feet moving in unison and shots of the gunmen moving into position. This camera work gives the dance an explicitly militaristic quality. Bill Whelan's energetic music, intensified by the use of drums, emphasizes the synchronized and escalating tempo of the dancers' feet. The film explicitly links the movements and music of Irish dance with the covert actions of the paramilitaries, thus aestheticising their act of violence.

I want to examine in detail the sequence of shots that lead up to the scene's final explosion. The leader of the ambush shouts 'Let's go!' as he jumps into a waiting car with his weapon disguised as a musical instrument that is casually slung over his shoulder. This exclamation triggers the image of the dancing girls. Their feet pound the floor in a pleasing display of precision beats, which correspond to the images of the gunmen's feet as they run into position. Interestingly, the dancers, like the masked gunmen, remain faceless. The tempo escalates as the dancers begin to perform more intricate choreography and the gunmen uncover their weapons to take aim. The following sequence of inter-cutting involves a close-up of the shoulder-held rocket launcher, with its long narrow neck ending in a rounded tip. After this weapon is swung into position, the film cuts to the dancers' legs. This time the image is held in freeze-frame as they perform a kick-step, which reveals their girlish white undergarments. This crotch-shot is directly followed by the firing of the missile and the explosion. In the split-second after the blast, the camera cuts back to the dancers: they are released from freeze-frame to pound an affirmative beat into the ground.

In this scene, dance is certainly implicated in the violence and in the IRA's effort to establish authority over and mobility within occupied territory. The dancers are positioned as the terrain on which the battle is staged. With their use of cinematic techniques such as freeze frame and slow motion, the filmmakers may also be referring to the restrictions on physical mobility enforced by the British government. In such terms, the dancers' movements are fixed on both sides: the body's motion is silenced by violence as the IRA bomb creates a blast that interrupts the scene, forcing the girls to run for cover. The dance is disrupted, but the cinematic narrative fully incorporates the dancers' movements into the choreography of the attack. By doing so, the film suggests that even forms of cultural resistance such as Irish dance may also become targets for violence, and asks about the extent to which the dancers are innocent victims of this military struggle, casualties of its violence.

In his poignantly written film *Dance Lexie Dance* (1997), Dave Duggan suggests that dance can be a force of personal as well as political conflict. The film portrays a Protestant father coming to terms with his daughter's desire to learn Irish step dance. When she asks why he does not want her to learn the dance he quickly exclaims, 'Because we don't dance!' His response acknowledges the perceived differences between Protestant and Catholic culture: one steadfast and somber, the other wild and unruly. Yet, at the film's conclusion, the father proudly witnesses his daughter's performance of an Irish step routine. The film's unspoken message suggests that dance is a way of moving beyond the traumas of the past. In *Dance Lexie Dance* and *Some Mother's Son*, then, dance is a metaphor for action, indicating that movement may focus political concerns and route them in a new direction.

In a parallel gesture, dance has been consistently invoked by those involved in the negotiations surrounding the Good Friday/Belfast Agreement as a metaphor for political progress. In the past five years, the rhythm of the parades and the process of the negotiations have often echoed one another as politicians engage, retreat, move forward, or stand their ground. Each gesture, whether on the parade route or around the negotiating table, has been scrutinized for meaning and significance. My own observation and analysis suggests that references to the mass movements of parading figured prominently in descriptions of the political orchestrations that led to the Agreement, while the language of dance offered a way of articulating the intricate political maneuvers needed to negotiate its finer points.

A political cartoon illustrating Brian Groom's 26 June 1999 editorial in the *Financial Times* dramatized the tensions between the Loyalist parades and the peace-talks by portraying both marchers and politicians as bodies that shared a common political and spatial path (Groom). The illustration depicts the leaders of the four main political parties involved in the negotiations for peace in Northern Ireland: the Ulster Unionist Party's David Trimble, Sinn Féin's Gerry Adams, Britain's prime minister Tony Blair and Ireland's taoiseach Bertie Ahern. They are shown sitting around a negotiating table, pointing fingers at one another as the document labeled 'peace process' literally comes apart on the table. In the background, the Orange Order marches toward them in full parade attire.

The cartoon can be read as implying a number of things: that the peace-talks are 'road blocks' on the path of powerful loyalist groups such as the Orange Order, or that the marches and the conflict they generate seriously threaten the progress of the political negotiations. As both interpretations suggest, the peace-talks and the parades often occupy the same political ground. While the image references a symmetry between the conflict generated by the parades and conflict surrounding the political process, it also highlights two distinct ways of moving toward a resolution. The diplomatic group discusses a political document at close range, while the parading masses display large banners as they march in strict militaristic choreography. The politicians sit at a roundtable in an instance of highly orchestrated political choreography. The marchers move forward en masse, their faces unidentifiable, their power in their numbers and their collective identity, while those at the table are clearly recognizable figures who must deal directly and individually with one another.

In an early reference to the difficult stages of pre-negotiations, Peter Brook, the British Secretary of State to Northern Ireland at the time, illustrates a kinesthetic connection between parades and politics in his rhetoric:

> As a consequence of the Anglo-Irish agreement, the unionists had elevated a tactic into a principle, not being prepared to co-operate at all because of the way they had been treated. And they effectively advanced, with drums beating and banners flying, into what was essentially a blind alley. (quoted in Bloomfield, 7)

The Unionist politicians' resistance to transformative political action prior to the negotiations was enacted on the parade route by the intransigence of the Loyalist marchers.

If the peace talks and the parades were partners in a strained political dance, both threatened to come to a standstill during the summers of 1995 and 1996. The Loyalist/Unionist standoff at Drumcree and their refusal to meet or even recognize the legitimacy of local residence groups reprised the Unionist strategy of political non-engagement with Sinn Féin (and, ironically, paralleled Sinn Féin's refusal to take their seats in Parliament). These obstructionist tactics had proved successful in attaining goals on the parade route and were implemented around the negotiating table, prompting one journalist to declare that 'storming out is the war dance of Ulster politicians' (quoted in Jenkins, 81). Whether on the parade route or at the table, Ulster hardliners waged war through physical resistance as the political parties aligned with the Orange Order translated the physical resolve of the marchers into a political strategy.

The difficulties of the marching season in Northern Ireland often correspond to the tensions played out behind closed doors at Stormont. Inside, language dances around the issues; outside, parade supporters and resident groups physically embody that struggle for power. The clichés often used to describe the negotiations are not incidental: path to peace, road to reconciliation, route to negotiations, first steps or road block, cul-de-sac, dead end, impasse. *New York Times* reporter Warren Hoge cites exactly such an image used by Trimble: 'We ... have boxed the IRA into a tactical, moral and political cul-de-sac' (4). The physical vocabulary of the parades offered the public, media, and politicians a metaphor for what was happening in the political arena.

The events of Drumcree heightened the already tense environment of the talks and put pressure on politicians to maneuver their parties into less entrenched positions. Some politicians had already begun to look for ways to facilitate greater flexibility between the parties by altering the format of the talks. During a series of earlier negotiations, Assemblyman Seamus Close commented on the disadvantages of the large meeting format: 'There was ... a situation of people playing to the gallery, and the more bodies there are and the bigger the gallery, the more likelihood there was of people taking entrenched positions' (quoted in Bloomfield, 187). As was clear from previous clashes over parades, confrontations between large groups of people were not the way forward. Senator George Mitchell has described trying to work past the roadblocks presented by the layout Close describes. He replaced the large meeting format with smaller plenary session discussions to facilitate a more workable and less hostile environment (Mitchell, 61). When all the political parties finally came together to witness the signing of the Good Friday/Belfast Agreement, Senator Mitchell notes, the spatial dynamic of the room had been intentionally altered:

> The shape of the table was changed from square to rectangular, to take up less room. That made it possible to let in some of the hundreds of members of parties who had come to witness history in the making. The place was packed with people standing in a solid mass. (181)

As the party members drew together, they physically affirmed their willingness to work together in a shared government.

However, Mitchell uses a static image. The immobilized mass in the room recalls the large blocks of bodies standing on the parade route; it references a body politic that will stand together but has not begun to move together. Once the agreement was drafted and voted on it was more than a document; it became a call for action. The finer points of the deal still had to be resolved, placing strategic importance on the wording, timing, and sequencing of movement during this stage in the process. These post-Agreement negotiations became a series of intricate duets between reluctant partners. Accordingly, media reports emphasized choreography as a tactic for approaching the post-Agreement negotiations over the timing of arms decommissioning, the demilitarization of Northern Ireland, policing, and the early release of political prisoners. As the negotiations turned toward the finer points of the Agreement, references to dance and to the movements of individual bodies proliferated, displacing the pre-Agreement talks' use of the physical rhetoric of the parades.

In August 1998, four months after the Good Friday Agreement, a political cartoon appeared in the *Derry Journal* that alluded specifically to the need for 'choreography'. David Trimble and Gerry Adams are drawn in caricature, their small bodies dwarfed by gigantic heads. Adams has his arm outstretched toward Trimble, who is sitting down with his arms folded. The words above Adam's head read, 'Would you care to dance, Mr Trimble?' In the background, the doors of the Northern Ireland Assembly remain shut. The caption 'Choreography ...' frames the scene.

The oversize heads point to the importance of the figures' political personas, and their body language suggests that the two hesitant partners must engage with one another in a formal dance. According to the cartoon, Trimble must decide whether to engage with Adams, while Adams is shown eagerly initiating a partnership as the apparent leader of this dance. Will they dance? What kind of dance will they do? Will Trimble join in? In the following years the two politicians would alternate between who led and who followed in step.

The language of choreography was so consistently deployed as a mode of intervention to help move difficult talks forward that one reporter directly questioned its utility as a possible solution for a stalled negotiation process:

> It is a truth universally acknowledged that no peace process can survive without forward momentum. There has been a lot of talk about 'choreography' in this process ... But can choreography resolve the decommissioning impasse? (de Bréadún)

Seamus Mallon, deputy first minister and member of the SDLP, more optimistically referred to choreography as a means to achieve resolution on the issue of weapons: 'The solution to decommissioning lay in the form of words, a timetable, choreography and a change of atmosphere' ('Still room'). His comments suggest that choreography can provide a form of predetermined schedule that will create a plot for action. Others also believed that choreography could resolve the decommissioning impasse: 'what is now at stake in Northern Ireland is no more than an issue of timing; of political choreography; of who is to move first' (Fitzgerald). As face to face discussions became inevitable, choreography became the way to engage, allowing politicians to adopt more intricate political positions in the process.

Pre-agreement debates over decommissioning soon focused on the intricacies of how to define 'sequential'. One commentator offered a strategic plan:

> In theory the choreography could be that Mr Trimble calls a meeting of the
> Executive, and the decommissioning body Chairman, John de Chastelain,
> announces that the IRA has decommissioned (perhaps destroyed Semtex in
> the presence of an international observer) … (Purdy)

These examples demonstrate that those involved sought a way to move politicians toward one another and across the political divide. Choreography, the scoring of dance in space and time, offers a way of conceptualizing movement as script for action. Dance historian Susan Foster has written persuasively on the significance of choreography in generating cultural codes and conventions: 'Choreography presents a structuring of deep and enduring cultural values that replicates similar sets of values elaborated in other cultural practices …' (5). When understood in these terms, terms clearly reflected in the examples discussed here, choreography becomes a powerful way to think through the relation between individual movements and social actions, between the human body and the body politic.

More specifically, the need for a political choreography at the negotiating table reflects the importance in Northern Ireland of attending to the larger 'social kinesthetic', defined by Randy Martin as 'a sentient apprehension of movement and a sense of possibility as to where motion can lead us', a sense 'that amounts to a material amalgamation of thinking and doing as a world-making activity' ('Dance and its Others' 36). Dance, in short, is a form that embodies the tensions and possibilities within the broader social and political configurations of Northern Ireland.

For this very reason, movement metaphors have continued to assist analysts and politicians in their conceptualizations of Northern Irish politics. Journalist Gene McKenna characterized the series of strategic maneuvers executed during a critical juncture in the talks as the 'political tango': 'When it comes down to the serious question of "tangoing" with political opponents, it all invariably revolves around the vital question of trust' (2). It is not surprising that McKenna referred to tango in illustrating the necessity and difficulty of establishing political trust, for tango embodies this very tension in bodily terms.

Tango has been described as a dance of domination and surrender between lovers, rivals, or enemies. Tango movements perform this history in steps that both resist and invite a partner's embrace. Dance scholar Marta Savigliano has written on the social and political origins of tango as a mode of resistance against colonial forces and as a vehicle for subverting sexual and political dominance: 'Tango is a practice already ready for struggle. It knows about taking sides, positions, risks. It has the experience of domination/resistance from within' (17). A photograph of David Trimble adjacent to McKenna's article seems to have caught the party leader in a moment of weight change or perhaps a tactical shift in his position toward Sinn Féin. As the headline for the accompanying article declares, he is 'Doing the Trimble'.

> After yesterday's roller coaster ride at Stormont, a special dance has already been invented in honor of the North's First Minister. It's called 'The Trimble'. You know the one. One step forward, a twirl or two, and then two steps backward. At least that was the way it was looking last night, after a day in which David Trimble appeared to have left the dance floor altogether. (1)

Here Trimble is the reluctant dancer performing a sequence of steps that move him cautiously toward his political opponent, circle, and finally take him back to his original stance.

The photograph registers Trimble's reaction to Adams's renewed commitment to disarm the IRA: he was knocked off his centre by the statement and struggled to find his feet as the political ground shifted beneath him. Prime Minister Tony Blair had declared the IRA's move 'seismic', directly invoking the movement of the ground itself. McKenna cites Adams' comment in the same article: 'We want to deal – we want to jump together with the Unionists … We want to work with them, not against them' (1). Perhaps for the first time since the beginning of the peace process the prospect of substantive negotiations seemed imminent. Adams's statement that he wanted to 'jump together' with the Unionists illustrates the challenges of political choreography. Perhaps it is a question of learning to move not in unison, but together, side by side, but with different steps. As political leaders become more familiar with one another and begin to perform the rituals of public office, they must find a choreography that will productively engage them in the push and pull of politics.

The communities of Northern Ireland must also participate in this choreography. Both aspects of political choreography that I have considered – the mass movements of parades and the individual movements of dance – must be mobilized in the pursuit of social and political stability. An example of this occurred in December 2000 in Belfast during President Clinton's visit to Northern Ireland. After a day of tense meetings with political leaders from both parties, President Clinton was to address a crowd of six thousand gathered at the Odyssey Arena in Belfast. While people waited, the song 'Brown Eyed Girl' by Van Morrison came blaring over the speakers, prompting the politically and religiously diverse audience to jump to their feet to do 'the wave'.

What was remarkable about this performance of the wave was that people had gathered to hear a political address about overcoming sectarian conflict, but first the crowd, including the politicians in attendance, joined together in spontaneous movement. One journalist reported that, 'as the wave began working its way around the indoor stadium, Northern Ireland's best known figures – as well as some of its *stiffest* – joined in' (Lacey, A10; emphasis mine). The movement of the wave created a momentary community that transcended Northern Ireland's political immobility. This diverse audience moved together: collectively standing up, sitting down, sharing a kinetic energy.

An idea in action, the wave demands individual *and* social fluidity to offer a danced expression of community, flexibility, and inclusiveness. To participate in this choreography one must join in the group action while also articulating individual gestures. The wave thus registers an image of Northern Irish society that draws on both individual agency and the collective power of the social body. Martin's 'social kinesthetic' is important here, for these bodies in motion suggest the way forward: prompting the community not just to stand together, but to act together.

Seamus Heaney also envisioned a 'cure' for Northern Ireland's troubles arriving in the shape of a wave, as told by the chorus in his version of *The Cure at Troy*:

> History says, Don't hope
> On this side of the grave,
> But then, once in a lifetime
> The longed-for tidal wave
> Of justice can rise up
> And hope and history rhyme. (77)

The crowd at the Odyssey Arena performed Heaney's promised 'tidal wave' as a sea of bodies rising and falling together, a society free to choose among many identities.

Viewing the recent political process in Northern Ireland through the lens of dance and choreography contributes to a broader understanding of politics and brings an increased attention to those forces which energize and motivate social change. Dance offers a language for articulating political formations that are non-verbal, but that are nonetheless in dialogue with discursive modes of communication. I advance this idea to encourage scholars, artists, activists and politicians to acknowledge movement as a vital and transformational element in our society.

WORKS CITED

Bloomfield, David. *Political Dialogue in Northern Ireland: The Brook Initiative, 1989–92*. London: Macmillan, 1998.

'Choreography … '. Editorial cartoon. *Derry Journal* August 1998.

de Bréadún, Deaglán. 'DeChastelain's flexibility best hope to end of impasse'. *Irish Times* 20 February 1999.

Duggan, Dave, screenwriter. *Dance Lexie Dance.* Dir. Tim Loane. BBC Northern Ireland / Northern Ireland Film Commission / Raw Nerve, 1997.

Fitzgerald, Garret. 'Former ties to US in question'. *Irish Times* 22 May 1999.

Foster, Susan Leigh. 'Choreographies of Gender'. *SIGNS* 24.1 (1998): 1–34.

George, Terry, dir., Jim Sheridan, prod. *Some Mother's Son.* Castle Rock / Columbia TriStar / Sony, 1996.

Groom, Brian. 'Marching toward the abyss'. *Financial Times* 26 June 1999.

Heaney, Seamus. *The Cure at Troy: A Version of Sophocles' Philoctetes.* London: Faber, in association with Field Day, 1990.

Hoge, Warren. 'Ulster Protestant leader wins a key vote'. *New York Times* 29 October 2000: 4.

Jenkins, Richard. *Rethinking Ethnicity: Arguments and Explorations.* Thousand Oaks, CA: Sage, 1997.

Lacey, Marc. 'Clinton, in Ulster, confronts warring passions head on'. *New York Times* 14 December 2000: A10.

Martin, Randy. 'Dance and Its Others: Theory, State, Nation and Socialism'. Unpublished essay, 2001.

—. *Critical Moves: Dance Studies in Theory and Politics.* Durham: Duke UP, 1998.

McKenna, Gene. 'Doing the Trimble – one step forward, a twirl, and then a few steps back'. *Irish Independent* 30 July 1999: 1–2.

Mitchell, George. *Making Peace.* New York: Alfred A. Knopf, 1999.

Purdy, Martina. 'Will it be peace or war for the IRA?'. *Belfast Telegraph* 15 February 1999.

Savigliano, Marta E. *Tango and the Political Economy of Passion.* Boulder: Westview Press, 1995.

'Still room for compromise, claims Mallon'. Editorial. *Belfast Telegraph* 2 March 1999.

Visions or nightmares? Murals and imagining the future in Northern Ireland

BILL ROLSTON

Introduction: Imagining community

Benedict Anderson's well-known and important insight into our understanding of political identity is that community is imagined. It is all too easy to take this as a smug dismissal of such phenomena as nationalism and ethnicity, and in doing so to conclude that political group identities are created out of nothing, probably for manipulative and narrow-minded reasons. Gellner puts this view forcibly when he concludes that 'Nationalism is not the awakening of nations to self-consciousness; it invents nations where they do not exist' (169).

Anderson himself rejects Gellner's position (Anderson, 6), and I wish to follow him in this regard. To talk of community as imagined is to state no more or less than that such identities as nationalism and ethnicity are social constructs. This is straightforward, mainstream sociology. Identities are not presumed to fall fully formed from the heavens to be donned by people like a suit of bespoke clothing. Rather, people need to make sense of their world and in doing so place an order on the chaos of events, thereby forging and acknowledging a shared sense of belonging together. Of course, this has frequently had disastrously negative consequences; as Ignatieff makes clear, belonging all too often is accompanied by blood. There is consequently endless scope for sceptics to evidence the downside of belonging. But at root what is involved is quite simply an attempt by people in groups to make sense of their world.

In doing so, they draw on certain elements of 'cultural capital' (Bourdieu and Passeron). For a start, they can refer to a myth of origin. Again, the phrase is open to different interpretations. Myth can be read as a cynical attempt at propaganda to fool masses of people. On the contrary, I am using it to refer to stories or social explanations which have an epic or heroic character. It is one thing to say, for example, that our ancestors one day just happened to end up in this place and here we are all these years later. But if we wish to celebrate, and thereby reinforce, our sense of community, it is more inspiring to tell tales of our ancestors overcoming countless odds and fighting fierce foes in order to establish a foothold. The point is not whether this rendition is true or false; such epics serve to highlight the group's need to represent its unique-ness. Again, this can be used as a weapon against those who are not of the group. But in itself a myth of origin is simply an expression of what might be termed ethnic pride.

That pride can be rehearsed through various cultural practices – a common lan-guage, historical narrative, religion, sport, or literature. Let me reiterate that there is nothing inherently negative in celebrating such communal culture. Of course, the ever-present danger of parading one's own sense of belonging is the exclusion, by force if necessary, of others. Ethnic pride is obviously built on a vision both of the group's past and of its future. Such a vision is a necessary element of communal solidarity and belonging. But where there is political conflict between the group and others on the outside, one person's vision can become another's nightmare. Cultural practices which from one angle appear merely as celebration thus become part of the battlefield.

The purpose of this essay is to examine a selection of political wall murals in the North of Ireland in the context of the above argument. Loyalists have been painting wall murals for a century, and republicans for only a third of that time. Through these cultural artefacts they articulate their political hopes and fears, their view of their own identity, their hopes of their past and future, and the political obstacles which they see facing them currently or in the future. In the abstract, the murals might be viewed simply as expressions of ethnic identity and pride, non-threatening and ultimately neutral as regards their assessment of others outside the ethnic group. But of course, in the real political world no such abstraction is possible. The murals emerge from the tripartite political conflict between Britain, Irish republicanism, and Ulster loy-alism; consequently, they are an integral part of that conflict. That said, for the most part, the murals of each side do not talk directly to the other side. Instead, each side's murals are about political mobilisation within their respective communities, about 'drawing support' (*DSi, DSii, DSiii*).[1] In that sense, they are intended more as a form of political education or reinforcement than as megaphone propaganda. But they are inevitably visible from across the political divide in the North. Given that, the vision of one set of muralists can be read by the other side as threat or nightmare.

Global connections

Republicans began seriously painting murals during the 1981 hunger strike. At vari-ous points thereafter the muralists were required to explain quite complex political

1 *DSi* refers throughout to Rolston, *Drawing Support* (1992); *DSii* to Rolston, *Drawing Support 2* (1996); and *DSiii* to Rolston, *Drawing Support 3* (2003). Examples of photographs of murals from all three publi-cations can be viewed on <http://cain.ulst.ac.uk>.

developments visually and to mobilize the republican community accordingly. For example, the previous republican approach to elections in the North had been one of abstention: 'Don't vote' or 'Vote for us and if we win, we will not take our seats'. But following the electoral successes of prisoners like Bobby Sands, Sinn Féin's electoral strategy moved into top gear. One task for republican muralists was to convince the possible sceptics or ditherers in the republican community that the ballot box was as powerful a weapon as the armalite (for a photograph of one such mural, see *DSi* 3). In this regard the muralists were at the forefront of political thinking, and in some cases one step ahead of elements of republican public opinion.

Another such instance occurred after the ceasefire of 1994. Preliminary talks and negotiations led eventually to elections for a devolved Assembly in the North. The Assembly and its power-sharing Executive, if and when established, were to meet at Stormont, a building which for seventy years symbolized one-party unionist rule and British involvement in the North, and as such a major obstacle on the way to the republican goal of a united Ireland. As Sinn Féin contested the elections, their constituency had to be convinced that going to Stormont was not a denial of past ideals or a recognition of British or unionist domination. Again the murals captured this complex message in striking ways. For example, one took the statement of James Craig, the first prime minister of Northern Ireland, and negated it: 'A Protestant parliament for a Protestant people no more'. A group of republican youths was depicted with tricolours and ropes pulling down the statue in front of Stormont of one of the main architects of the Northern Ireland state, Edward Carson (see *DSiii* 1). No such event has ever occurred during the peace process, so the imagery referred not to people's everyday experience but to television images they had seen a decade earlier of statues of Stalin and Lenin being demolished in Eastern Europe.

The ease with which republican muralists have been able to 'borrow' images from elsewhere says much of the way in which republicanism is a broad church. As O'Dowd has pointed out (165), Irish nationalism in the nineteenth and twentieth centuries managed at various points to ally itself with every major contemporary political ideology, from fascism and communism to feminism. Loyalism, on the other hand, has a uniqueness about it which leads to splendid isolation. It has tendencies towards both the right of the political spectrum and the left, a current example of the latter being the positions held on a number of social issues by the Progressive Unionist Party, which is linked to the Ulster Volunteer Force (UVF). However, overall loyalism does not sit easily with any contemporary political ideology. It is situated on the narrow ground of maintaining the status quo ante: 'What we have, we hold'; 'No surrender'; 'Not an inch'. The slogan of the other major loyalist paramilitary group, the Ulster Defence Association (UDA) sums up the ultimate goal – 'Quis separabit', or 'Who will separate us?' – as does the central tenet of all loyalist paramilitaries that their *raison d'être* is defence: of the Union with Britain, of Protestantism, and of what remains of Orange-unionist ascendancy (Brown). Loyalism thus leaves very little space for borrowing images from elsewhere; it is hard to imagine, or paint, a vision of the future in which sacred cows are dismantled when one's whole existence is about protecting those cows.

Take the question of how republicans and loyalists respectively identify with other political developments and struggles globally. Republicans have painted murals in which they have identified with the political struggles of political groups such as the Palestine Liberation Organisation (*DSi*, 50) and the Palestinian people generally (*DSiii*, 32), the African National Congress (*DSi*, 58), the South-West African People's Organisation in Namibia (*DSi*, 49), the Sandinistas in Nicaragua (*DSi* 59), the Basques (*DSiii*, 32), and the people of East Timor (*DSiii*, 33). Individual African American and Native American activists like Martin Luther King (*DSiii*, 34), Malcolm X (*DSiii*, 31), and Leonard Peltier (*DSiii*, 33) have also been portrayed on the walls. More generally, republicans have been adept at taking the discourse of international human rights on board in their local campaigns about issues such as prisoners and victims of state human rights abuses. What is involved here is quite clearly a process of political imagination: republicans have concluded that the struggles of people elsewhere against colonialism, imperialism, and state repression are like their own, that the resistance evident elsewhere resonates with their own. From the point of view of those who make such global connections, it is not necessary to examine these claims with the forensic eye of a political scientist.

For loyalists, there is much less scope to feel at home in a wider political world. True, as the Intifada raged during 2002, many loyalist areas sported Israeli national flags; but the suspicion must be that this was more about getting back at republicans for displaying Palestinian flags in support of the Intifada rather than an identification with Israel per se. It could be argued that, as settler societies (Clayton), 'Ulster' as imagined by loyalists and Israel have much in common. But the loyalists themselves made relatively little of the connection; while there were some slogans such as 'Loyalists support Ariel Sharon', there were no murals attempting to make the link.

In general terms, civil rights and human rights discourse does not come easily to loyalism (although human rights discourse has been used tentatively in one mural in East Belfast, as depicted on the front page of the *Belfast News Letter* for 1 February 2002). Partly this is because the discourse has already been occupied by republicans, but there is a deeper explanation in that such discourse has often been used globally as a form of resistance to oppression and status quo. In contrast, the rhetoric of 'no surrender' unfortunately more closely resembles the attempts of dominant and oppressive groups – like the National Party in South Africa – to hold on to power.

These two factors – a general unease with the rhetoric and visual representation of resistance and liberation, and the fact that such means come more easily to their republican rivals – has meant that the vocabulary of political expression has been severely reduced for loyalism. On one occasion, loyalists organised a long march from Derry to Portadown in support of Orange marchers seeking to parade through the nationalist Garvaghy Road area of Portadown. They likened their long march to the one organised from Selma to Montgomery by Martin Luther King in March 1965. A colleague of King, Donald Payne, leader of the black caucus in the US Congress, objected: 'These [Orange] marches have been symbols of intimidation and oppression for Northern Ireland's Catholic minority for over 100 years – to characterise them now as civil rights marches is particularly grotesque' (quoted in Erwin). The same Congressman had no difficulty speaking publicly in nationalist and republican West Belfast, openly drawing comparisons between the situation of the local people and that of African Americans (Payne).

On occasion some loyalists have made connections with those at the far right of the political spectrum. Football matches in Northern Ireland (and indeed Scotland) have been for many years a site of sectarian chanting and display (Sugden and Bairner). From time to time there have been strong racist overtones as well. Thus loyalist supporters have carried banners supporting Combat 18, a British fascist group whose name refers to the first and eighth letters of the alphabet, 'A' and 'H', the initials of Adolf Hitler. And in 2002 a mural appeared briefly which was both disturbing and politically confused. Under a series of flags indicating loyalist identification with Canada and South Africa were a swastika and the letters 'KKK'. Interestingly, the only flag available seems to have been that of the new South Africa, the rainbow nation, rather than that of the old apartheid regime, which one suspects would have been more suitable.

Myths of origin

Another way in which to identify one's ethnic position, rather than by comparing oneself to others, is to stress one's uniqueness, and in particular the supposed origins of the group which confer distinctiveness on it. Again there is a stark difference between republicans and loyalists in the ability to tap into such myths of origin.

For republicans, there is a vast pool of mythology and history on which to draw. The Gaelic revival in the late nineteenth century led a number of writers and scholars to rediscover and re-translate the epic tales of the Celts, full of heroic deeds, fierce battles and brave warriors. (Similarly, Mexican nationalists in the first two decades of the twentieth century were involved in the re-imagining of their roots as pre-Colombian rather than colonialist. Three internationally famous painters – David Siquieros, Diego Rivera and Clemente Orozco – painted huge murals as their contribution to this revival; see Charlot.) More recently, the brawny Celtic warriors, together with comely maidens in diaphanous clothing, have provided great scope for at least one Irish artist, Jim Fitzpatrick, to represent these epic characters and tales. Fitzpatrick's representation of mythical heroes such as King Nuada and battles such as that at Moytura were faithfully reproduced in a number of republican murals (*DSi*, 57).

One of the greatest of Irish origin myths is the Táin (Kinsella). Briefly, it is the story of a raid by Queen Mebh of Connacht on Ulster in order to steal a large bull. She is helped in her task by the fact that the warriors of Ulster have fallen under a spell which renders them incapable of fighting – all except one, Cuchulain, who was born outside Ulster. He single-handedly takes on Mebh's army and thwarts her plans. In another tale, Cuchulain is mortally wounded in battle, his dying wish that he be allowed to die upright. Cuchulain was greatly admired by the Gaelic revivalists in general, and in particular by Padraig Pearse, one of the key instigators of the Easter Rising of 1916, who clearly identified with Cuchulain's noble if ultimately futile armed struggle. Another 1916 combatant (and later Taoiseach and President of the Irish Republic), Eamon de Valera was likewise drawn to Cuchulain and was instrumental in having a statue of the dying hero, cast by Oliver Sheppard, placed in the General Post Office in Dublin, the headquarters of the Easter Rising (Rolston, 'From King Billy to Cuchulain'). The republican credentials of the image are thus second to none, and accordingly it has appeared in a number of contemporary republican murals (see *DSiii*, 25).

Loyalists have much more difficulty with constructing a myth of origin. One ingenious attempt has been the move to reconstruct Cuchulain as a loyalist. In this reading, Cuchulain is seen not as a Celt, but as a Cruthin or Pict, a member of a racially distinct clan resident in the northern part of Ireland and in Scotland prior to the Celts' domination of Ireland overall. In this reading, Mebh was a Celt and invaded Ulster to steal the bull. Only one man was available to defend Ulster: Cuchulain (Adamson, *The Cruthin* and *The Identity of Ulster*). In effect, Cuchulain was the first loyalist paramilitary. This reworking of the traditionally republican myth was supported by the officer cadre of the UDA and first saw the light of day in mural form at Freedom Corner in East Belfast in 1991; amazingly, the image was an exact copy of the Sheppard sculpture in Dublin's General Post Office (*DSii*, 17). Later loyalist Cuchulains have repeated this image (*DSiii*, 45), while others have represented the supposed proto-loyalist almost in the style of heavy metal iconography. The problem of the Sheppard image in particular is that rank and file loyalists do not easily identify with it. One young UDA member interviewed by McAuley concluded that the image at Freedom Corner was 'awful fenian looking' and dismissed the attempts by UDA leaders John McMichael and Andy Tyrie to fashion an Ulster, as opposed to British, identity: 'That's John and Andy's baby and I don't take much to do with it' (95).

Painting history

History is another source of imagery for republican muralists. In the first instance, this is of course the history of republican struggle: the United Irishmen in 1798, Robert Emmet in 1803, and the 1916 Rising have all been depicted at one time or another (*DSi*, 60 and *DSiii*, 53). This is potentially a very narrow and organisational take on history. But representation goes beyond this to wider depictions of the history of the nation. Often the story is presented in terms of victimization – the Penal Laws and the practice of Catholicism (*DSiii*, 26), the Famine (*DSii*, 59) – but there is also a sense of pride, survival, and resistance, as in the depiction of the hedge schools of Penal Law days (*DSiii*, 26).

For loyalists, the dominant image in murals for many years was the iconic figure of King Billy, depicted on his white horse at the Battle of the Boyne in 1690. This image spoke eloquently of the annual attempt by unionism to represent itself as one big happy family, a task which succeeded relatively successfully up until the 1960s. More recently, as the disunity within unionism came to the fore, the King Billy images have been fewer, although they still appear from time to time (*DSiii*, 54). With the fading of King Billy images, to all intents and purposes, loyalist imagery was bereft of historical references. In the last few years there has been a partial turnaround in this respect, with murals depicting scenes such as the 1641 massacre, when the Catholic natives rose up against the Protestant settlers; the closing of the gates of Derry by thirteen apprentices in 1689, which sparked off a prolonged siege; or Cromwell's involvement in Ireland, depicted not merely as a military but also as a religious campaign (*DSiii*, 52–3).

All of these have appeared in UDA-controlled areas. For the UVF, historical reference has been an easier task through the years. Representing themselves as the direct descendants of the original UVF, formed in 1912 to oppose Home Rule, they have had wide scope to reproduce images of the time, such as Edward Carson or the motorised division of the UVF (*DSi*, 11). The palette becomes even wider when one remembers that with the outbreak of World War I the UVF joined the British Army en masse as the 36th Ulster Division, which was decimated at the Battle of the Somme in July 1916. Silhouetted figures of soldiers from the Great War or images of the troops going over the top frequently appear in murals in UVF-controlled areas (*DSiii*, 51). The UVF has appropriated this whole historical period as an exclusive rather than a pan-loyalist one. Interestingly, loyalists seem more comfortable on the terrain of such sectional or organisational history; thus, the UDA has depicted in murals its own involvement in the Ulster Workers' Council Strike of 1974 (*DSiii*, 55).

This approach to history in organizational rather than wider or 'national' terms arises from a number of causes, not least the tension within loyalism as to whether their nation is Britain or Ulster. The neglect of wider history is also due in part to a crisis within Protestant areas as regards formal education. Figures released by the Greater Shankill Partnership reveal that, while 42% of 18-year-olds in Northern Ireland overall go into higher education, in Protestant West Belfast the figure is 0.7%. In 1986–7 in the Greater Shankill area, only 4% of primary school children passed the 11–plus examination for admission to grammar school, compared to a Northern Ireland average of 21%. In 1987–8 the total number of children in the Greater Shankill area who passed was a mere 11; in 1988–9 it was 13. In 1992, 37% of secondary school children on the Shankill left school without any GCSE qualifications.

More specifically, young loyalists, as community workers in unionist areas will confirm, are remarkably ignorant of history. To cite one example: two teenage UDA members questioned by McAuley had not heard of the plantation of Ulster (94), and one of them suggested that their ancestors had arrived in Northern Ireland 'just before World War One'. Although the blame for this lack of knowledge may be partly laid at the door of an education system which fails all working class children, there is also a sectarian differential apparent within Belfast's working class. This is because there are other popular sources of historical knowledge available to the young outside of authorized school curricula. Thus, young nationalists have the opportunity to be aware of a vibrant culture with deep historical roots, no matter how mythical, where a similar opportunity is not available to young unionists. The potential of remedial work in this respect emerging from their schools is sometimes missed. Thus young people on the Shankill have easy access through school trips to Fernhill House, a local museum in what was formerly the house of a wealthy business family. Although purporting to present Shankill history, the museum in fact focuses almost entirely on military history (Fernhill House). This is compounded by UVF murals on the streets that concentrate on the Battle of the Somme and other murals that depict the Battle of the Boyne. Consequently, it is difficult for the young unionist to see history as anything other than an account of past wars, and two in particular.

There have been attempts recently to go beyond such a narrow take on history through the commissioning of murals by the Ulster Scots Heritage Council. These murals represent the first serious attempt at political education by loyalist muralists. As well as admonitions to speak the language and celebrate the culture, there are lessons in the history of the Ulster Scots migration to America and the successes of descendants of those emigrants, such as frontiersman Davy Crockett, whose ancestors came from County Derry, and the 16th President, James Buchanan, whose parents came from County Donegal (*DSiii*, 56–8).

'*I am who I say I am': contemporary republican and loyalist identity*

For republicans, the contemporary political terrain is a familiar and exciting place. Having been relegated to the status of second class citizens in the history of Northern Ireland and before, they have a quiet confidence that time is one their side. They have come in from the margins and have a long view of politics, believing that continuing to call on the political system to deliver on its promises while at the same time highlighting the contradictions involved in the attempts to so deliver will eventually be to their benefit. Their vision is of a united Ireland, once fought for solely through military means and now deliverable through politics. This sense of confidence and ethnic pride is evident in many of the cultural products of republicanism, including murals. One group working in the broad republican tradition in Derry in the 1990s – Derry Frontline – put it in poetic form in their manifesto for a festival in 1989. The title of the festival was '20–20 Vision', the purpose being to view how far Derry had progressed in the two decades since the beginning of the conflict, and to envision the Derry that local people would want two decades in the future.

> When children are more valued than bombs
> And they read the books we write.
> When women are valued more than work
> And our homes are no longer prisons.
> When justice no longer huddles in cells
> Nor strangers crouch armed in our streets.

When we own our own cities and fields,
We will know the meaning of freedom.

Until such time
The cries of our cities and the groans of our land
Will be the songs of our wisdom,
Our poetry of anger and hope.
Until such time
Our wonderful murals and graffitied thoughts
Will be our street newspaper,
Our uncensored judgement and art.

But while you dance to our songs
And market our lives,
Read our lips:

We are the people of struggle,
Ours is a culture of change.   (Derry Frontline)

Confident, focused, determined, and articulate republicanism – this is the stuff of loyalist nightmares. Loyalists, in contradistinction, feel beleaguered and 'unsettled'
(McKay), fearing that the modern world holds little place for their ideology and that
republicans do indeed have time on their side. This is a recipe for desperate measures,
for implosion through endless turf wars and intra-loyalist feuds, or explosion through
attacks on nationalist areas and personnel that are not easily represented as rational or
productive, even in their own terms. Take the Holy Cross saga during 2001 and 2002:
republicans were able to paint a mural which represented loyalist attacks on schoolchildren passing through a loyalist area on their way to school each day as resembling
the racist attacks on African American schoolchildren in Arkansas in 1957 (*DSiii*, 9).
In addition, they could quote to powerful effect the promise of the Good Friday
Agreement that everyone had 'the right to live free from sectarian harassment'. But
there is no mural on the loyalist side which attempts to explain why they were attack-
ing primary school girls each morning with taunts, fireworks, and bags of urine. Take
also the issue of Orange marches: republicans can clearly represent in murals why they
don't want triumphalist marches in their areas (*DSiii*, 8), but there is little explanation in loyalist murals of why they need to march where local people do not want
them. One of only three murals referring at all to Orange marches in fact seems to

confirm the republican charge of triumphalism: 'Where our music is welcomed, we will play it loud. Where our music is challenged, we will play it louder' (*DSiii*, 38).

In a similar vein, loyalist artists often seem to be clutching at the straws of popular culture, representing the giant Finn McCool (*DSiii*, 45), Bugs Bunny (*DSi*, 24), the dog Spike from the 'Tom and Jerry' cartoon series (*DSi*, 23), Bart Simpson (*DSii*, 18), and Fred Flintstone as loyalists. The last of these has not yet appeared on a mural, but you can buy t-shirts with the slogan: 'Yabba dabba do, any taig'll do'.

Conclusion

Republicanism can easily represent itself as visionary, but loyalism has a more difficult task in doing so. Republicans have no problem articulating the future: they see change as being on their side. Loyalism, on the other hand, can only see itself as under threat; the very confidence of republicanism seems to say to loyalism that the future of loyalism is that there is no future for loyalism. In such a situation, it is very difficult to have an inspiring vision of the future. Muralists benefit or suffer because of these wider scenarios. There is no political contortion or cognitive dissonance involved in republicans identifying with and borrowing imagery from other nationalist, anti-colonial, or anti-imperialist struggles in the world. For their part, loyalist muralists cannot put into visual form aspirations which are not there; hence the continuing popularity of paramilitary images even in the midst of a peace process. What is involved is not a failure of will but of vision. The future, with the prospect of the continuing electoral success of Sinn Féin or a Catholic majority in the population within a generation, is a frightening country for loyalism.

WORKS CITED

Adamson, Ian. *The Cruthin: A History of the Ulster Land and People.* Newtownards: Nosmada Books, 1974.
—. *The Identity of Ulster.* Belfast: Pretani Press, 1982.
Anderson, Benedict. *Imagined Communities: Reflections on the Origin and Spread of Nationalism.* Rev. ed. London: Verso, 1991.
Bourdieu, Pierre, and Jean-Claude Passeron. *Reproduction in Education, Society and Culture.* London: Sage, 1977.
Brown, William. *An Army with Banners: The Real Face of Orangeism.* Belfast: Beyond the Pale Publications, 2003.
Charlot, Jean. *The Mexican Mural Renaissance, 1920–1925.* New Haven: Yale UP, 1963.

Clayton, Pamela. *Enemies and Passing Friends: Settler Ideologies in Twentieth-Century Ulster*. London: Pluto Press, 1996.

Derry Frontline. *The 2020 Papers*. Derry: Derry Frontline, 1989.

Erwin, Alan. 'US chief's fury at long march'. *Irish News* 1 July 1999.

Fernhill House. <http://www.belfastcity.gov.uk/heritage/pdf/hooffront.pdf>.

Fitzpatrick, Jim. *The Book of Conquests*. New York: E.P. Dutton, 1978.

——. *The Silver Arm*. Dundalk: De Danaan Press, 1983.

Gellner, Ernest. *Thought and Change*. London: Weidenfeld and Nicolson, 1964.

Greater Shankill Partnership. <http://www.shankillpartnership.com/about.htm>.

Hobsbawm, Eric, and Terence Ranger, eds. *The Invention of Tradition*. Cambridge: Cambridge UP, 1992.

Ignatieff, Michael. *Blood and Belonging: Journeys into the New Nationalism*. London: BBC Books, 1993.

Kinsella, Thomas, trans. *The Táin*. London: Oxford UP, 1970.

McAuley, Jim. *The Politics of Identity: A Loyalist Community in Belfast*. Aldershot: Avebury, 1994.

McKay, Susan. *Northern Protestants: An Unsettled People*. Belfast: Blackstaff Press, 2000.

O'Dowd, Liam. 'Intellectuals and Political Culture – a Unionist-Nationalist Comparison'. *Culture and Politics in Northern Ireland 1960–1990*. Ed. Eamonn Hughes. Milton Keynes: Open University Press, 1991. 151–73.

Payne, Donald. *Urban Regeneration and the Struggle for Civil Rights: An African-American Perspective*. Belfast: West Belfast Economic Forum, 1996.

Rolston, Bill. *Drawing Support: Murals in the North of Ireland*. Belfast: Beyond the Pale Publications, 1992.

——. *Drawing Support 2: Murals of War and Peace*. Belfast: Beyond the Pale Publications, 1996.

——. *Drawing Support 3: Murals and Transition in the North of Ireland*. Belfast: Beyond the Pale Publications, 2003.

——. 'From King Billy to Cuchulain: Loyalist and Republican Murals, Past, Present and Future'. *Éire-Ireland* 32.4–33.2 (1997–98): 6–28.

Sugden, John, and Alan Bairner. *Sport, Sectarianism and Society in a Divided Ireland*. Leicester: Leicester UP, 1993.

The Troubles told to children

CELIA KEENAN

This paper sets out to examine the ways in which the Northern Ireland Troubles have been reflected in literature for children. It asks why children's literature seems to be less successful than adult literature in this area. In particular, it examines the depiction of elements that are thought of as particular components of those Troubles: religion and religious groups; political allegiances; military and paramilitary groups. It focuses on three elements of story – characterization, point of view and closure – in an attempt to understand some of the problems in these narratives. It concludes that the particular anxieties linked to writing for children and the publishing context are significant factors in the failure to create a convincing literature for children about the Northern Ireland Troubles.

In the thirty years since the Northern Irish Troubles began, one striking feature of much of the writing for children on the topic has been a tendency to stereotype the different groups involved. In particular, a form of religious stereotyping is common. Sometimes this takes forms that might be seen as relatively benign. For example, it is a commonplace in the work of writers such as Joan Lingard and Peter Carter that Catholics have remarkably large families (the size is usually remarked on) and are somewhat feckless and unthinking. Protestants conversely have small families and are industrious in a rather dull and uncreative way. At times, however, this form of stereotyping is less benign. An example of this can be found on the opening page of Carter's novel *Under Goliath* (1977), where the narrator, a Belfast Protestant, describes the Orange order in an ironic eleven-line paragraph, which ends with this assertion: 'To make sure the Protestant religion stays on top in Northern Ireland, is what the Orange order is all about, although it's even money whether most of its *members know as much about religion as you do* '(5, italics mine). The sneer of the outsider is visible in that final comment, which, incidentally, is far from an accurate account of members of the Orange Order, many of whom are also pillars of their religious communities (hence the dilemma experienced by the Church of Ireland about permitting the use of Drumcree church for a service by the Order during the Garvaghy Road controversy). Members of the Orange Order are frequently described with contempt in children's literature about the Troubles. They are usually presented as boorish, stupid, and sometimes dangerous.

Cultural and religious icons, whether of Protestants or Catholics, are rejected with equal and unconcealed contempt in Carter's novel. When the narrator and hero, Alan Kenton, visits the home of his Catholic friend Fergus Riley, he is struck by the proliferation of religious images in the house, and then by the flying ducks on the wall, which were such a common decoration in working class households. He subsequently recalls that his Loyalist uncle Jack Gowan's home is decorated in a similar way, with the same flying ducks on the wall but with images of the Queen of England and the Royal family. The Catholic father and the Protestant uncle equally represent ugly forms of bigotry. At the end of the novel, in an emotional rejection of Northern Ireland, the adult Alan says that 'Rage fills my heart … A rage at Gowan, and Mr Riley whose name was good in the Falls. A rage at plaster saints and brass Vaticans and barren chapels … a murderous rage at the waste and the folly of it all' (168). Each religious image here is qualified by a derogatory adjective that implies a visceral ideological rejection of the culture of Northern Ireland. In much of this literature for young people, even when religious icons are presented positively – as is a silver crucifix in the very recent book by Stewart Ross, *Everything to Live For* – they are merely used as a handy signifier of religious allegiance. In *Everything to Live For*, a kindly, upper-middle-class, middle-aged surgeon called Mr Robinson is revealed as Catholic by a little silver crucifix he wears around his neck. The fact that it would be unlikely for a man in his position and of his age, Catholic or not, to be thus decorated is not allowed to get in the way of a useful icon or an epiphany in which a young Protestant girl suddenly realizes that not all Catholics are murderous. In general, it seems fair to say that Catholic and Protestant children would find very little in these books that reflects their religious beliefs and culture in any positive or realistic way.

The depiction of opposing legal and illegal military and paramilitary forces, such as the Royal Ulster Constabulary, the Garda Síochána, and the British army on the one hand, and the IRA and Loyalist paramilitary groups on the other, raises some interesting questions. Surprisingly, perhaps, the police forces, both the northern RUC and the southern Garda Síochána, receive pretty unsympathetic treatment from a number of writers. This is most obvious in Catherine Sefton's *Frankie's Story* (1988) and in Mark O'Sullivan's *Silent Stones* (1999). It could be that these writers are simply reflecting the common adolescent suspicion of police forces. There is relatively little attention paid to the Protestant paramilitaries, except in Catherine Sefton's *The Beat of the Drum* (1989), which is one of the very few books that convey a sense of a communal life lived in a working-class area. In this book the reader is invited to understand a loyalist community and the forces that lead young people into paramilitary organizations. A character such as the hero's uncle can be at once loyal, lovable, and deeply prejudiced. Sefton avoids stereotyping along religious and social lines and displays a notable absence of the contempt that shapes other narratives.

In contrast with the fairly scant attention paid to loyalist paramilitaries, depictions of members of the IRA are prominent in a substantial number of these books. In particular, many books about the Northern Troubles stereotype republican paramilitaries *either* as unfeeling sociopaths who literally betray their own mothers or children, *or* as gullible victims of cynical godfathers (John Quinn's *One Fine Day* [1996], and Gillian Cross's *Wolf* [1990] exemplify this tendency). It is highly unlikely that residents in working-class nationalist areas of Northern Ireland would recognise in these stereotypical figures the people they support and for whom they vote. Tom McCaughren's *Rainbows of the Moon* (1989) deserves particular attention in this regard.

Rainbows of the Moon is a boy's adventure story set on the fringes of a battle between members of an IRA active service unit and an undercover British army unit. Two boys from opposing republican and unionist backgrounds observe and become embroiled in the action. There is a radical difference in register between the depictions of IRA and British Army soldiers. The IRA men are cold and impersonal: the two main IRA characters are nicknamed The Hawk and The Professor. The Hawk has cold blue eyes, and spits rather than speaks. The reader is left in no doubt that the narrator, who ascribes false and envious motives to his actions, disapproves of his narrowly nationalist views. Every thought and view attributed to the Hawk is mediated by the intrusive narrator with phrases such as 'he saw himself', 'he bitterly considered', 'he believed' (this latter repeated several times): 'He was from Northern Ireland or the occupied six counties as he himself called them ... He saw himself as a member of a nationalist minority which by a stroke of a British pen has been corralled against their will into a small corner of Ireland with a loyalist majority'. He has waged war on 'What he bitterly considered to be the forces of British Imperialism' (73). The Hawk has one trait which might at first seem to humanise him: he does not want the boy protagonists to get hurt in the battle with the British army. However, that humanity is diminished when the narrator repeats on at least two occasions that his concern is only because one of the boys comes from a republican family background. He is not at all concerned for the safety of the children as children. The second important IRA character, called The Professor, is an explosives expert from a middle-class Dublin family background: he wears rimless glasses; he seems to have no interest in anything except explosives; he looks old and grey; his paramilitary comrades find his explanations tedious and difficult to understand. In the case of these IRA characters, no detail suggests a life lived. There are no references to wives or children or broader family loyalties, nor are there any references to favourite foods or memories or dreams.

This is in marked contrast to the depiction of the corresponding British soldiers. Their leader, SAS Sergeant Striker, has brown eyes: 'A very dark brown, behind which all feeling and emotions were carefully guarded' (39). Guarded emotions are very different from the cold lack of feeling exhibited by the IRA men. Striker can be witty and sarcastic, and he cares for his men and rewards their efforts with good food, saying 'Jolly good. Have whatever you fancy. You've had a hard day' (77). The men cook up an aromatic and appetising curry which domesticates them and renders them attractive to the young reader. Another soldier, Private Brown, is the British soldier with whom the reader is invited to empathize most. He expresses a love of simple domestic pleasures in language that sounds like that of a boy: 'What I'd love now is fish and chips, chips not soggy but fresh and crisp, salt and vinegar, a nice bit of smoked cod, all nicely wrapped and almost too hot to eat' (76). This statement is designed to make the young reader sympathize with Brown, as is his evocation of an ideal leisurely Sunday morning having fun with his children and his declaration that he likes a few pints of bitter and 'a laugh with my mates' (78). This is an image of a warm, fun-loving, sensual man, loyal to his wife, children, and mates, a trustworthy man. He is the single victim of IRA aggression in the novel. The author has evoked such sympathy for him that the reader can feel only outrage when he is killed in a booby-trapped explosion, his 'disintegrating body framed in a blinding flash' (96).

In contrast to the hard-line political views of the IRA men, the British soldiers express a somewhat bemused and disinterested confusion about Ireland. One of the soldiers says, for example, 'It's funny alright how some of them are prepared to fight us to stay British and the others are prepared to fight us because they say they're not British' (131). What emerges is the common colonial view of the natives as irrational people who defy common sense. This view is not challenged or mediated by the narrator. The role of the British army in Ireland is never subjected to the kind of scrutiny with which the IRA and indeed the Loyalism and Nationalism of the boy protagonists are examined.

The British Army similarly provides a moral frame in Peter Carter's *Under Goliath*. The two boy protagonists, Alan and Fergus, grow up and join that army. Fergus is killed in an unnamed foreign field and his boyhood friend cradles his dead body. It is interesting that Carter places the final army action outside of Northern Ireland, and that he strains credibility somewhat by putting nationalist Fergus into the British army. It is the army and not Belfast that claims his life. However, that army is sentimentally treated as the locus of friendship, loyalty, and love. Carter's story is the one

in which the British army receives its most sentimental treatment, but as I have indicated with the case of McCaughren, such sentimentality is not unique. I have come
across only one exception to this tendency to romanticise that army. That is the short
story 'A Letter from Wally' by Jan Needle, which takes a startlingly unsentimental
view of the role of the British army in Northern Ireland and of army life in general.
The intransigence of its subject matter is reflected in its rather unlikely epistolary
form. The whole story is narrated in a letter from a soldier to his former schoolteacher, a person of radical humanist values. The way in which the inhabitants of
Northern Ireland are described is utterly depersonalized. Violence to women and to
the native Irish is not avoided. The soldiers' misogyny is unsparingly scrutinized, as
in the following examples: 'The Kraut birds were awful, right? ... The Protestants are
appalling and the Catholics are worse ... we should just piss off and leave them to it'
(71). The reader is given to understand that the soldier-narrator has probably killed
an innocent child. There is no attempt at self-justification. There is, however, a per-
vasive sense of the inevitability of terror. This is an interestingly honest and entirely
English view of Northern Ireland as an alien space. The central theme of the story,
though, is less a comment on Northern Ireland as such, and more a critique of the
class structure of British society and the inequalities of its education system, which
push young men into the army.

Just as Jan Needle's story presents a more challenging and less benign view of the
British army's role in Ireland than is usual in most books for young people, Mark
O'Sullivan's novel *Silent Stones* presents an unusually complex view of republican violence and culture. *Silent Stones* is set in the Republic of Ireland in the late 1990s, in
the period after the IRA ceasefire, the Good Friday Agreement, and the subsequent
bombing in Omagh. Its protagonists are members of a republican family with a long
tradition of IRA membership. In the beginning of the novel, O'Sullivan describes an
old IRA man, Eamon Wade, and a crazed ex-IRA man on the run, Razor McCabe,
in clichéd and stereotyped terms. They live in squalor, are motivated by bitterness,
and have no real political vision. Of Protestants, Eamon Wade says 'They deserved
everything they got. Them and the bloody Brits, propping up a rotten, corrupt state
for fifty years' (25). However, despite a seemingly clichéd beginning, the novel develops in an interesting and complex way. The stereotyped characterization is deepened
even in the case of the crazed Razor McCabe. All the characters have an interior life,
a personal history, memories, loves, and affections. There is an emphasis on learning
from past mistakes and responding to changed circumstances. In the aftermath of
the ceasefire, it is difficult for republican activists to accept that the war is over. By
the end of the novel Eamon does so, but loses his life in the process. The hero of the

novel, teenager Robbie, must come to terms with the tragic history of his republican family. The fact that he has an English girlfriend who is a new-age traveller and whose grandfather had been an arms dealer provides an interesting point of contact with the larger world, which is not entirely innocent of the terrible events that have happened in Ireland. The book even subverts the cliché that young men are drawn into violent action by sinister godfather figures when the elderly Eamon confesses that he first joined the IRA because his enthusiastic younger brother had already done so.

However, in spite of the fact that this book presents a more complex understanding of republicanism than many of the others discussed above, it also shares certain tropes with them. Here, as in so many other books, the hero has rejected the republican values of his family. In *Under Goliath, Frankie's Story, The Beat of the Drum*, and *One Fine Day*, the heroes – whether from republican or loyalist backgrounds – have all rejected their own political loyalties before the beginning of the novel. This means that they cannot be seen as truly representative of their respective communities. They function more as extensions of an omnipotent authorial voice. In a sense, then, they are token insiders, but the point of view they reflect is rarely that of an insider. There is an interesting problem with the point of view in almost all these novels. The imagined reader is almost invariably someone from outside Northern Ireland. Thus, in *Under Goliath*, Peter Carter's narrator says 'Now in case you think that the Orangemen are maybe a body of greengrocers or whatever, let me tell you they are no such thing' (5). The 'you' addressed is very clearly not Irish. No one in Ireland, north or south, would require this explanation.

A similar example can be found in *Frankie's Story* by Martin Waddell, published first under the pseudonym Catherine Sefton. The eponymous Frankie, the narrator, comes from a nationalist background. On the first page of the novel, she describes 'four RUC men, that's Royal Ulster Constabulary, our cops' (Sefton, *Frankie's Story*, 1). This explanation is clearly directed to a reader outside Northern Ireland. This also leads Sefton/Waddell to sound one of the few false notes in his 'troubles' trilogy because it is unlikely that a girl from a nationalist ghetto would describe the RUC as 'our cops'. The point of view is almost invariably that of distanced observer in these narratives. The loss of authenticity is a serious one.

Another problem that limits authenticity in these books is that of closure. Many of these novels end with the hero or heroine leaving Northern Ireland and going to live in either Britain or the Republic of Ireland. Bill Rolston has analysed this pattern as it pertains to the works of Carter and Lingard (41). The pattern has continued to a certain extent in *Frankie's Story* and *One Fine Day*. However, there have been novels which have subverted this pattern. For example, it is deliberately resisted in the third of Sefton/Waddell's Troubles novels, *The Beat of the Drum*, where the hero Brian decides very firmly to stay in Northern Ireland within his own community, largely because he is needed and loved there. As he says, 'If I go, and all the others who think like me go, what'll happen to the people who are left' (Waddell 138). At the end of *Silent Stones,* Robbie, the hero, makes a similar decision. In Carlo Gebler's *Frozen Out* (1998), the process of emigration from Northern Ireland is reversed. The heroine, a young English girl from London, comes to live in Northern Ireland and manages to come through the trials of adolescence in much the same way as other young people in the western world. The difficulties of living in a divided community are not minimised. At the same time, other aspects of life are less sinister than in the London where the family formerly lived. This is most graphically illustrated when the heroine's young brother gets lost. His parents' worst fears about his safety are not realised and kind neighbours go out of their way to find him and bring him safely home. From the works of Sefton/Waddell, Gebler, and O'Sullivan it is possible to argue that writers, particularly in recent years, are responding (albeit in a limited way) to political change and acknowledging the complexities of the situation in Northern Ireland. However, in much of this writing there is still a sense of authors mediating the reality of life in Northern Ireland for imagined wiser and more sophisticated readers in London or Dublin.

There are many possible reasons why this is the case. One might be an inordinate sense of moral responsibility felt by writers in view of the serious nature of the northern conflict. Mary Beckett, Joan Lingard, Tom McCaughren, Martin Waddell, and Sam McBratney have all expressed this in a variety of ways (Coghlan and Keenan 112). Beckett, who has written so superbly about the Troubles in her seriously neglected adult novel *Give Them Stones,* has not written directly on the topic for children. She says 'My adult stories had frequently been described as "uncomfortable" and I have always thought that children's books should give them comfort and security ... in writing about Belfast it is even more necessary to create a safe protected life for them' ('Ulster Dimension: Branching Out', 20). A number of writers have found that they can confront the problems more successfully through the lens of historical fiction, as McCaughren does with *In Search of the Liberty Tree,* where two boys, one from each side of the political divide in Ireland, become embroiled in dangerous and violent situations against the background of the 1798 Rebellion in Ulster.

Sam McBratney, another writer from Northern Ireland, explains why his treatment of the Troubles is for the most part indirect or in the background (as is the case in his novel *You Just Don't Listen,* formerly published as *Put a Saddle on the Pig*): 'Writers should be careful of tackling the raw aspects of life here without being able to call on the complete range of adult concepts which help us make sense of what is happening. Themes involving violence, bigotry, sex, religion and death are bound to be tricky territory for writers of children's books' ('Ulster Dimension: Writing and Imagining', 18). Interestingly, in the same article McBratney says that his book *The Chieftain's Daughter* 'was written for the joy of writing'. *The Chieftain's Daughter* has all the themes listed by McBratney as difficult to handle: violence, bigotry, sex, religion, and death. They are handled very skilfully and forcefully. It is tempting to think that it is the fact that the novel is set in the time when Christianity was in its infancy in Ireland, and not in contemporary Northern Ireland, that makes this possible.

Robert Dunbar, however, in his essay 'Children's Fiction and The Ulster Troubles', points to the fact that writers write better about the Troubles when they resort to metaphorical obliqueness rather than literal directness. He also points out that the insistence on impartiality at all costs can 'come very close to saying nothing at all' (83). The implication of what he says is that writers can be so concerned with balance and impartiality that one is left with unreality.

The best writings for adults about the troubled world of Northern Ireland seem free of the kind of constraints that children's books reveal. Among them, a novel such as *Give Them Stones*, or a play such as Gary Mitchell's *In A Little World of Our Own* (1998), are works which in their different ways speak out of their respective Catholic and Protestant communities, and do so without apology, without the sense that they are mediating Catholic or Protestant, nationalist or loyalist experience for some wiser, more rational 'Other' in London or Dublin. That they have managed to do this without giving offence to those outside their respective communities is a tribute to the skill of their writers. They convey, without apology, the sense of what life is like in Catholic and Protestant communities: they extend understanding, they speak from within. Perhaps greater courage is required on the part of children's writers and publishers, greater artistic integrity with less moral and political correctness. Courage and artistic integrity might free them from the constraints of political correctness so that they could dispense with some of the stereotyping outlined above. In the actual world of Northern Ireland, not all Orangemen are stupid boorish bigots, not all IRA men are unfeeling monsters, and not all members of the British army are decent chaps engaged in perfectly rational disinterested action in Ireland. The only legitimate voice is not the secular liberal voice from London or Dublin. Artistic integrity would ensure that more of the truth was told to children, and then the children of Northern Ireland might possibly recognise their own world in books about their home place.

As I have shown, many established children's writers from Northern Ireland have expressed serious anxiety, coming close at times to despair, about treating the Troubles for children. Perhaps if they could publish in and for their own communities that sense of hopelessness would diminish. For the surprising fact is that none of the writers under discussion, whether from the nationalist or unionist tradition, has had his or her work published in Northern Ireland because, until very recently, there was no publisher of children's books in Northern Ireland. This is in spite of the fact that Northern Ireland has a number of very prestigious adult publishing houses, and that in the Republic children's books are published not only in Dublin but in Cork, Galway, and Mayo. When a book was required to represent Northern Ireland for the recent European Picture Book Project, the book chosen was *War and Peas*, which was published in Great Britain and written by Michael Foreman, who is not from Northern Ireland (Cotton, 45). By and large, writers from the unionist tradition publish in London and writers from the nationalist tradition publish in Dublin. They write with a Dublin or a London reader in mind. The Dublin and London political and artistic establishments share a common distaste for passionate loyalism, passionate nationalism, and the unapologetic expression of intense religious feeling.[1]

Only a tiny handful of children's books have been published in the last ten years in Northern Ireland. The most important of these was an optimistic attempt to create an Ulster-based alphabet book, *An Ulster Weans A–Z* (McIvor). It bravely attempts to represent icons of both communities in a positive way. It doesn't patronise or demonize either community. Children from both communities could find reflections of their culture in it. Blackstaff Press published it with the Cultural Traditions Group, whose aim was to encourage an understanding of cultural diversity. As its title, which includes the Ulster Scots word 'wean', suggests, it attempts to give expression to the language and culture of Ulster. It tries to take the harm out of cultural and political difference by daringly and wittily juxtaposing icons of opposing traditions. P is for Pope, for example, and Q is for Queen. In a crowded comic-strip-style text, rival pieces of graffiti nudge each other. The Red Hand of Ulster, with 1690 underneath (associated with the loyalist UVF), sits beside a harp on a green background and the barely discernible words 'Tiochfaid ár Lá' (a slogan associated with the Provisional IRA). There is nothing random about the way images are placed. The graffiti referred

1 This is attested to by a wide range of recent events: the embarrassed laughter of an Abbey Theatre audience during the first production of Mitchell's *In a Little World of Our Own*, when, at a particularly tragic moment, one of the characters, an evangelical Christian, exhorted the others to pray; the surprised and amused reaction in the Dublin media to the fact that at the 2003 All Ireland football final the two Northern Ireland teams (Armagh and Tyrone) and all their supporters sang the entire Irish national anthem without interruption (Humphries 1); and the recent controversy in that most liberal of British newspapers, *The Guardian*, when the columnist Julie Burchill described a St Patrick's Day parade in London as 'A celebration of a religion that condemns contraception, abortion, divorce and the right of a woman to be a priest' (5).

to are both depicted on the wall of Mussenden Temple in County Derry, a temple built by the radical Church of Ireland Bishop Hervey in the eighteenth century. Hervey supported both the American War of Independence and the idea of Catholic emancipation in Ireland. He permitted Catholics to celebrate Mass in his temple once a week (Connolly, 239). It is tempting to imagine that he might have appreciated both the republican and the loyalist icons on the temple wall, unlike contemporary writers for children who contemplate them and the traditions they represent with horror or contempt. (Ironically, while there is at present an attempt being made to repair the temple, it teeters on the edge of a cliff, an appropriate metaphor for the newly devolved state.) The book was written during the first IRA cease-fire and its optimism is understandable. In its good-humoured way it is respectful of both traditions. It is one of very few books for children published in Northern Ireland. In my view those two facts are inextricably related. Nothing published for children outside Northern Ireland on the subject of the troubles has been as respectful of the cultures of Northern Ireland as this little book.

Subsequently, a small number of picture books has been published by Discovery Publications, based in the nationalist Crumlin Road in Belfast. They include Declan Carville's *Valentine O'Brien Irish Dancer* (2000), assertively in the nationalist tradition with its cult of traditional Irish dance and its Celtic decoration, and *The Incredible Sister Bridget* (2001), which has a kind of super-nun as its heroine and which is unapologetically Catholic in its iconography. Even though these books are naively written and somewhat crudely illustrated they are very much to be welcomed as a first attempt to publish for nationalist children from within their own community. They are a sincere reflection of Catholic and Nationalist feeling. They would never have been published in London or indeed in Dublin. One hopes that they may promise more and better publications for nationalist/republican/Catholic children and for unionist/loyalist/Protestant children: books which will respectfully reflect their lives and cultures.

Only when writers from both communities begin to have their work published in Northern Ireland for a readership of children in Northern Ireland will we have a literature that reflects the realities of life in Northern Ireland. Then, perhaps, the distortions imposed by the rules of political correctness and by the need to please outside audiences, distortions of characterization, of point of view, and of closure may be avoided.

WORKS CITED

Beckett, Mary. *Give Them Stones.* London: Bloomsbury, 1987.

——. 'The Ulster Dimension: Branching Out'. *Children's Books in Ireland* 8 (May 1993): 8.

Burchill, Julie. 'Dying Nine to Five'. *The Guardian* 20 Sept. 2003: 5.

Carter, Peter. *Under Goliath.* London: Oxford UP, 1977. London: Puffin, 1980.

Carville, Declan. *The Incredible Sister Bridget.* Belfast: Discovery, 2001.

——. *Valentine O'Byrne Irish Dancer.* Belfast: Discovery, 2000.

Coghlan, Valerie, and Celia Keenan, eds. *The Big Guide 2: Irish Children's Books.* Dublin: Children's Books Ireland, 2000.

Connolly, S.J., ed. *The Oxford Companion to Irish History.* Oxford: Oxford UP, 1998.

Cotton, Penni. *Picture Books sans Frontiéres.* London: Trentham Books, 2000.

Cross, Gillian. *Wolf.* Oxford: Oxford UP, 1990.

Dunbar, Robert. 'Children's Fiction and The Ulster Troubles'. *Proceedings of the 12th Annual Conference of the Reading Association of Ireland.* Dublin: Reading Association of Ireland, 1987. 74–91.

Foreman, Michael. *War and Peas.* London: Hamish Hamilton, 1974.

Gebler, Carlo. *Frozen Out.* London: Mammoth, 1998.

Humphries, Tom. 'All Ireland Final'. *Irish Times* 29 Sept. 2003: 1.

Lingard, Joan. *Across The Barricades.* London: Hamish Hamilton, 1972.

——. *The 12th Day of July.* London: Hamish Hamilton, 1970.

McBratney, Sam. *The Chieftain's Daughter.* Dublin: O'Brien Press, 1993.

——. 'The Ulster Dimension: Writing and Imagining'. *Children's Books in Ireland* 8 (May 1993): 18.

——. *You Just Don't Listen.* London: Mammoth, 1994.

McCaughren, Tom. *In Search of the Liberty Tree.* Dublin: Anvil, 1994.

——. *Rainbows of the Moon.* Dublin: Anvil, 1989.

McIvor, Philip, illus. *An Ulster Wean's A to Z.* Belfast: Blackstaff Press, 1996.

Mitchell, Gary. *In a Little World of Our Own.* London: Nick Hern Books, 1998.

Needle, Jan. 'A Letter from Wally'. *A Pitiful Place.* London: Andre Deutsch, 1984.

O'Sullivan Mark. *Silent Stones.* Dublin: Wolfhound Press, 1999.

Quinn, John. *One Fine Day.* Dublin: Poolbeg Press, 1996.

Rolston, Bill. 'Escaping from Belfast: Class, Ideology and Literature in Northern Ireland'. *Race and Class* 20.1 (Summer 1978): 41–62.

Ross, Stewart. *Everything to Live For: A Story from Northern Ireland.* London: Hodder Wayland, 2002.

Sefton, Catherine. *The Beat of the Drum.* London: Hamish Hamilton, 1989.

——. *Frankie's Story.* London: Hamish Hamilton, 1988.

Waddell, Martin *The Beat of the Drum.* London: Walker, 2001.

Language, memory and conflict: acts of interrogation

LIAM KELLY

In Ireland, there is a particular relationship between word and image that is, in many ways, endemic to the culture. Witness, for example, the British government's former banning of direct interviews with Sinn Féin representatives, so that we got a curious form of image and dubbing. And, of course, there is the word, the text, and the Bible in Protestant fundamentalism, where truth is revealed in the word. By extension, there is a suspicion of the visual, a suspicion that it may be 'wayward' and related to fancifulness. There are also the literary structural models of writers like Joyce, O'Brien, and Beckett. But what most of the artists considered in this paper share is the use of words as ways of rinsing up what is invested in the psychic landscape of memory.

The recent political and violent conflict in Northern Ireland has acted as a catalyst in the shift from a lyrical but potent pastoralism in the work of a previous generation of artists to a more searching intellectual and discursive art by the present generation of artists. There has been an intensive period of self-reflection and interrogation by artists on issues such as place, tradition, and identity. In this paper I will examine how artists – such as Michael Farrell, Willie Doherty, Paul Seawright, Rita Donagh, Michael Minnis, Patrick Ireland, Philip Napier and Shane Cullen – have deployed and interrogated language both orally and textually as a working strategy for engagement within the post-colonial context of Northern Ireland.

I: Michael Farrell

Michael Farrell's work is an historically important point with which to begin. Towards the end of the '60s, Farrell's work began to change. The political troubles in Northern Ireland had already begun, and Farrell's work, which to date had no political connotations, began to respond to the tragic situation in Ulster. A series of abstract works, his *Presse* series (1970–), which were purely formal studies, now began to take on meanings that put the formal elements of his visual vocabulary to the service of more politically significant and impelling content. What appeared like squelches of 'pop juice' in the earlier works now became blood; the once sterile language of the *Pressé* series became the passionate *Pressé Politique* (1973). Anonymity in the abstract works gave way to personal identity and political expression in more committed narrative works.

Variations on this theme continued to become more and more reflective on what it means to be Irish and an artist, rather than merely an artist. In *Une nature morte à la mode Irlandaise* (1975), we witness newspaper headlines of various tragedies in Northern Ireland, chopped up by the now fulminating *Pressé* elements and the use of witty and clever punning on the concept of *nature morte* in the deadly appropriate French title. In an interview in the *Irish Times* in 1977, Farrell reflected upon his artistic change:

> I became interested more in the literary aspects and less in the formal ... I've withdrawn from the international stream of art to a more human and personal style than before. I found in my big abstract works that I couldn't say things that I felt like saying. I had arrived at a totally aesthetic art with no literary connotations. I wanted to make statements using sarcasm, or puns, or wit, and all of these I could not do before because of the limited means of expression I had adopted. (quoted in Barrett, 14)

Farrell was, by now, living in Paris, and from what his new domicile had to offer, he chose to deploy the eighteenth-century French artist Boucher's painting of Miss O'Murphy (herself an Irish emigrant living in France, and one-time mistress of Louis XV) as a more potent symbol for the direction in which his artistic and personal concerns were leading. In one of this 'Madonna Irlanda' series, the artist lays out Miss O'Murphy like the chart of a cow in a butcher's shop, signifying the various butcher's cuts – 'gigot, forequarters, le cut, knee cap'. Here, by word-play, he both puns upon the name of the original artist, Boucher (meaning butcher in French), and poignantly comments upon the savagery of the political system, and upon its victims in the North of Ireland (knee-capping is a customary punishment carried out by the IRA for informers and the like). The artist himself has said of these paintings: 'They make every possible statement on the Irish situation, religious, cultural, political, the cruelty, the horror, every aspect of it' (quoted in Barrett, 15). One should add to his list the exploitation of women.

II: Willie Doherty

Considerations of language are central to Willie Doherty's practice. In his earlier work he superimposed text over images, one to subvert the other. The overprinting of words on image creates a compound, existential state, where contradictions, ironies, subversions are at work. In *The Walls* (1987), the artist arranges text to settle over sections of a horizontal panoramic view of Derry's Bogside area in daylight and the elevated, dark, inner side of the city walls from which we/the artist, the colonised/the coloniser take in the view and take up a position. *The Walls* lingers with the legacy of the colonized and the colonizer in its absences and presences. From the inner, walled city, captioned 'Within/Forever' (in loyalist blue), we survey the outer/other, the Bogside, captioned 'Always/Without'. Jean Fisher points to the fragility of the seeing/being seen relationship in *The Walls*:

> As we imagine that, with powerful lenses, we could penetrate the interiors of the facing windows, so we also become aware that those eyes may see us. Indeed, were it not for the presence of this gaze of the other we should not be able to assume the sovereignty of power that this position affords us. The seeing/being seen dyad is a question of both position and disposition: I see you in the place I am not. (1)

The Walls, then, deals with inclusion and exclusion, and Derry, in microcosm, reflects a siege mentality that is culturally endemic in Northern Ireland as a whole.

Doherty has also turned his attention to more recent examples of social and urban planning during the 1980s in Belfast. The Westlink dual carriageway, for instance, cuts a deep gorge into west and north Belfast, and cuts off deprived areas (both Catholic and Protestant) from the inner city to accommodate the easy flow of commuter traffic through the city. In his novel *Lies of Silence,* Brian Moore, who once lived near a section of the present Westlink, comments on class divisions in Belfast:

> For he had seen photographs of the pre-war city, orderly, ugly, Victorian. But when the war had begun a quarter of a century of civil strife had worsened, so that now, beneath the new motorways which crossed the city like slash marks on a map, the old heart of Belfast, those thousands of small dwellings which housed people whose highest ambition was a job in the shipyard or a mill, lay in a continuing plague of poverty, decaying without hope. (11)

In Doherty's *Strategy: Sever and Strategy: Isolate* (1989), we note the single barricaded footbridge crossing the motorway from Divis Flats, while in *Policy: Commitment* (1989) and *Policy: Investment* (1989) he compares policies of projected economic growth and city gentrification with the lingering nature of ongoing social realities. In these works, stubborn words form condemning compounds with the images and cannot be erased by the political rhetoric of promise.

From his audio/slide installation *Same Difference* (1990) to his acclaimed *The Only Good One Is a Dead One* (1993), the complexities of language, as mediated in the press and TV, and the related dangers of stereotyping as a barrier to understanding have driven Doherty in his early works. The dualities of perception, ideology, and mediation were developed in a different way in *The Only Good One Is a Dead One*. This work is a double-screen video projection installation. On one screen the artist uses a hand-held video camera to record a night-time car journey, while the second screen shows the view from inside a car which is stationary on the street. The accompanying sound track consists of the interior monologue of a man who is vacillating back and forth between the fear of being the victim and the fantasy of being an assassin. As does much of Doherty's work, this video installation operates by way of a series of binary operations. There is the double-screen viewing (compare his early use of the diptych in photographic works) and, as in 'The Walls', the seeing/being dyad (surveillance). There is also the violator/victim duplicity: guilt and innocence. As such, these series of double encodings allow for at least a double reading of his work, a necessary condition to avoid taking up the all too easy fixed position of a prejudiced view.

III: Paul Seawright

Paul Seawright's photographic works are another example of the transformative power of text on image. During 1987–8, he made a series of fifteen photographs based on visits to the scenes of various sectarian murders, or to the locations where bodies were dumped in the early 1970s, an intense period of sectarian violence. He did not give the series a title, but reviewers have always referred to them as the *Sectarian Murder* series.

The time interval of some fifteen years between murderous and creative acts was important to the artist, not only to ensure the religious anonymity of each victim, but also, in a sense, to indicate that the murdered were victims of being in the wrong place at the wrong time. By producing these photographic works 'out of time', the artist allowed for more objective reflection on the original violent events, while their considered re-construction 'in time' induced purposeful empathy with the victims and their circumstances. Using an old diary from his youth, which noted significant political events among the fairly quotidian entries, Seawright spent protracted periods of time at these sites, considering the meanings associated with their location. In some cases, he re-enacted the route taken from the place where a victim was snatched to the eventual spot of the murder or the dumping of the body. Such reconstructions of reality built up tensions within the artist, and elicited the lingering presence of grossly transgressive acts from the location. Each scene was photographed in colour from the victim's viewpoint, close to the ground. The lighting of each scene was controlled, which paralleled the forensic photographer's cold, stark approach.

These photographs, however, would remain merely interesting formalist studies if their accompanying text was not integral to their meanings. Seawright had researched original journalists' reports of these killings from local newspapers in Belfast, and had selected snippets of text from such reports to work with and to discharge their related images of any easy reading. These are composite works: the juxtaposition of image and text allows for one to play off the other. The text in relation to the image ties them down irrevocably to a place, a sub-culture, and a value system of violence.

One of these images views a roadside inn down low, from the illuminated grassy edge of the road. A general feeling of tension is engendered by the angle of 'shooting', the absence of people, and the gap created between the stationary car and the lorry about to pass the inn.

> Saturday, 16th June, 1973. The man was found lying in a ditch by a motorist at Corr's Comer; five miles from Belfast. He had been shot in the head while trying to hitch a lift home. (Seawright)

As an integral part of the work, this blunt factual text tells of the killing of this misplaced victim. It also seems to indict the pictorial vehicles, as the location becomes perpetually marked and troubled. Unlike TV news coverage of such killings, Seawright's works contain no reference to sectarian claims of justification or politicians' repudiations. The cold sparsity of the text unites with the concentrated absences in the photographs to sustain a resounding moral condemnation of any claimed political cause and its violent expression. Seawright's re-creation of these fateful routes and locations is a form of psychic mapping of the landscape's dark side.

IV: Rita Donagh, Michael Minnis, and Patrick Ireland

In his essay dealing with public art and locality, Luke Gibbons takes us into what Wittgenstein has called 'the rough ground' (16). For Gibbons, an acknowledgement of this is a necessary condition for a more open, less fixed sense of place, and public art projects have the capacity to 're-frame' experience – to draw out the 'rough ground' – of everyday experience. Recent decades have witnessed globally huge re-alignments of place and identities. Never has the need for map-making been more urgent, or the need for it to be under more scrutiny.

> 'Cartography' as the articulating sign system for the immense shifts taking place all around us between places, spaces and the subjectives which designate them as the location (or dislocation) of identity, requires an ever vigilant critical re-examination. (Rogoff, 144)

Many Irish artists, as elsewhere in other zones of conflict, have deployed 'mapping' (un-mapping/re-mapping) as a counter-cartography and critical strategy to interrogate social, political, and personal issues.

For Gibbons the map may open up new ways of seeing, but its diagrammatic disposition is restrictive in reflecting the cultural investments in landscape – the 'occlusion of time' (16). In her exhibition *A Cellular Maze* (1983), Rita Donagh reacted to the idea of the physical and graphic presence of the H-Blocks (Maze Prison) on the landscape, and considered the location of the H-Blocks in their proximity to Lough Neagh, with its associations with ancient Irish mythology. The artist also used the idea of the six counties as a territorial unit, or what she calls the *Shadow of Six Counties* (1973–), a shadow on the lung – the presence of the British? By exploring grids and various projections through a series of drawings, Donagh led one to *Long Meadow* (1982). Usually one sees aerial photographs of the Maze Prison, but here we see the blocks diagonally set across the canvas like a still from a German expressionist film – light creates the intense mood of this air raid.

Maps are also economical with the truth. In the early 1990s, Michael Minnis continued to be interested in how the city of Belfast reveals itself – how it is marked, denoted, and often denied representation for security reasons. He painted sections of aerial-view, ordinance survey-type maps of Belfast onto aluminium sheets. On these maps, security-sensitive buildings have been left blank by the mapmakers. As applied to the aluminium, these negative spaces allow the reflective aluminium to shine through; the gallery environment is thus recorded in this reflection. In some works, the blank of the original map becomes a cut-out in the aluminium and the artist attempts to re-invest these vacancies with meaning. In *Street Index* (1993), he attempts to reconstruct a street destroyed by violence, by using a Belfast street directory for names and occupations of former residents. These were interwoven with the map network as an attempted re-fabrication, as a way of offering resistance to loss.

While a number of Irish artists use maps, Patrick Ireland (aka Brian O'Doherty) is fascinated by networks, structures, mazes, and labyrinths. In 1985, at the Douglas Hyde Gallery in Dublin, he made *Purgatory*, part of an ongoing series of rope drawings. The source for *Purgatory* was Joyce's *Finnegans Wake* - a series of non-sentences of line words. He takes these line words and traces them as a network over a section of the map of Dublin (the Irishtown/Philsboro area). He then transposes this contrived grid into a 3–D rope drawing within the gallery space. On a central axis to this grid there is a table and a chair. Spread on the table we have the opening sequence of *Finnegans Wake* written on blotting paper by hand. On either side of the installation, there are phrases being sounded out from speakers. Around the walls is a series of ancillary drawings that indicate the thinking process behind the installation. He transposes ideas from one art form to another.

Ireland believes in ambiguity and paradox. On entering the gallery, the viewer sees a series of letter forms on the back wall: HCE, which stands for the Earwicker / Here Comes Everybody theme in *Finnegans Wake*. At first glance, the spectator thinks it is projected onto the back wall, but one later realises that it is painted onto the wall. More recently, Ireland extended this interest in illusion, perception, and ambiguity to the Ulster situation. *BIG H* (1989) dealt with an identity clash through the interaction of colours – orange and green. Where viewers to the exhibition stood, both physically and culturally, it may be speculated, would affect their perception of both the formal/colour interactions and the ideology at work. For unionists, orange would visually be drawn forward: for nationalists, green would advance. All Patrick Ireland's works (rope drawings, structural plays, et al.) deploy an urgent, tense geometry which invites participation/actuation. The viewer/performer is compelled to 'actuate' (i.e., bring into life) the framework geometry by bodily movement/involvement. His series of rope drawings, for example, as with *BIG H*, remain merely visual concepts, dormant until a critical positioning of the viewer 'actuates' and energises the installed spacial geometry.

V: Philip Napier

Philip Napier's art practice is not only an interrogation but a detonation of language around and through an axis of power. A recent work, *Gauge* (1997), commissioned and developed for the Orchard Gallery, was conceived as a two-part project. Part 1 occurred as an installation in the Orchard Gallery space, while part 2 was presented as a temporary site-specific public artwork in the Bogside area of Derry. Initially, the events of Bloody Sunday (the 25th anniversary was 30 January 1997) provided the contextual point of reference for this work. It was conceived against a backdrop of sustained calls for an apology from the British Government for the events of Bloody Sunday on 30 January 1972, when 14 unarmed civilians were shot dead by the British Army.

The installation consisted of fourteen audio speakers suspended by wire from circular dialed weighing scales – the traditional type you once saw in grocery stores. These speakers relayed a continuous litany of spoken apologies: 'I'm sorry … I'm so sorry … I'm sorry about that … Sorry … I apologise'. The sincerity of these apologies was 'measured' by the agitation of the needle on the face of the dial. The slipperiness of language – its ambiguous disposition, especially in colonial or conflict situations – was in effect being 'gauged'. The work evolved as a proposition that language alone cannot be adequate; indeed, that no measure of language can be enough because it is always contextual and conditional. It is a question of power relations and whether a bureaucratic apology could ever be enough to eradicate a communal wrong.

In part II, this work was reconceived and installed in a derelict Housing Executive dwelling in Glenfada Park in the Bogside. The installation faced a courtyard which was the site of some of the shootings and one of the last architectural remnants of the events of 1972, lingering now amidst widespread redevelopment. The work was installed as though in hiding in these largely unreconstructed derelict houses, and was encountered through torchlight amidst unsettling blanket darkness.

The central theme of these two presentations of the work focused on the value and nature of an apology. Who is apologizing and to whom? Can mere words be adequate? Are words measured, or can they be 'measured'? The discourse surrounding the problematics of the nature of apology echoes with the registers of colonial and post-colonial situations the world over. That year alone, to my knowledge, this debate about apologizing had stretched from Japan and its treatment of World War II POWs, to South Africa and its Commission for Truth and Reconciliation, to the Bosnian War Crimes tribunal in the Hague.

In *Gauge* it is not specified who is asking for an apology, who is apologizing, or to whom they are apologizing. This public and private experience is left to address the cultural and political baggage of its audience. The act of mediation here arises from its local and universal outreach. Tom McEvilley, who experienced at first hand this site specific work, acknowledges this issue of both local and global relevance in his catalogue essay on *Gauge*:

> Encountered in Glenfada Park, the piece seemed to refer to the Irish demand that the British apologise for Bloody Sunday. Indeed its appropriateness to the site – combined with its sense of dark hiddenness – was uncanny, almost eery. Still, as one listened, its resonances seemed to pass beyond the specific situation and approach the universal. Not only the British relation to the Irish seemed involved, but the relationship of all colonisers to all the colonised peoples everywhere. It reminded me of Hegel's parable of the Master and the Slave, from the second book of the *Phenomenology of Spirit*, where History is seen as a long slow shift of relationship through struggle, in which the antagonists' attempts to overcome one another through annihilation culminate in a mutual overcoming through a kind of absorption, a reception of the other as the negation which completes oneself. (6)

McEvilley raises two pertinent points here: firstly, the universal outreach of Napier's work beyond but extending out of the local, the immediately known; secondly, the role or possibilities of language in bringing about wholeness or resolution between colonized and colonizer, or resolution within a state of interdependence. In this he embraces (by way of Hegel) Homi K. Bhabha's 'Third space of Enunciation' – a necessarily ambivalent space.

VI: Shane Cullen

Like Napier, Shane Cullen is interested in the ramifications of language – its emotional, psychographic charges. Cullen's series of tabula-like texts, *Fragmens sur les Institutions Républicaines IV* began in Ireland in 1993 and were completed while on residency at the Centre d'art contemporain de Vassivière en Limousin, France in 1997. The work was exhibited there from February to April 1997. The complete ensemble of texts which form this monumental project were in turn exhibited for the first time in Ireland at Derry's Orchard Gallery, in December 1997. The work represents secret communications or 'comms' written by Irish Republican Hunger Strikers and smuggled out of the Maze Prison (the so-called H-Blocks) during the highly charged period of the hunger strikes in Northern Ireland in 1981. These hunger strikes, in which ten participants died, were mounted in an effort to establish political status for IRA prisoners.

In Cullen's representation of these comms, the emotional and fragile language of the private was graphically and in a proclamatory way introduced into the public domain of the polis – that which pervades both the physical and political space. The project consisted of 96 panels in a serial presentation of *fragmens*. These comms, handwritten by the artist, have been monumentalised in the act of representation, paradoxically by the handwritten process aping a mechanical process. On one level, interjection by the artist is located in this act of transcription. In the act of re-pre-senting these once-secret letters like a monument with a 'formal' text in the public domain, the artist opens them up to public scrutiny. This creative act draws parallels with the process-centred ritual of the early Christian scribes or Chinese calligraphers – in their activity of repetitive copying can be detected a striving after idealism. As such, Cullen's act of 'writing out' replicates the underlying ideal (national unity) sought after by Republicanism.

The title of the work is itself taken from a series of political ideological texts writ-ten by Louis Saint-Just at the height of the revolutionary period in France. In 1793–1794 Saint-Just wrote a treatise which was posthumously titled 'Fragmens sur les Institutions Républicaines'. The Saint Just text is formally laid out in sections, separately presented but interrelated. In this way it offered itself as a utopian model of how society could be structured both socially and politically. What appears to be an orthographical error, that is, *fragmens,* is in fact an accurate detail of the original Saint-Just manuscript. It is, actually, an archaic spelling of the word *fragments*, in common usage prior to the standardization of the French language. Cullen adopts the formal layout of the Frenchman's text for his artwork and thereby sets up ideo-logical correspondences between the respective Republican texts.

Cullen's work begs questions not only about the representation/re-presentation of text but its location in the 'polis'. The work looks like a public monument but is anti-monumental and as fragile as the language it represents. The strategy of mediation at work here, in one sense, is the opposite of Napier's in that it brings the public domain of the city monument into the contemplative domain of the art gallery. It is also body-related – not only to the bodies of those on hunger-strike but also to the body of the artist. Mike Wilson draws our attention to this in his catalogue essay on Cullen's project:

> This work, this monument which is more a representation of a monument than a monument proper, is marked by the trace of a particular body, the

body of the painter. It is further marked by the absent bodies, bodies reduced, erased and superceded by text. It is marked by their words, the words of dead men negotiating the terms and conditions of their death. (19)

In relation to these remarks by Wilson, it is worth recalling Maud Ellmann's insightful observation that the more the body becomes emaciated by a hunger strike, the more loquacious the person becomes – there is an urgency in the need to communicate: words spill out (72).

Conclusion

Two central and related issues are at the core of the conflict in the North of Ireland. They are place (the emotional ground/territory) and cultural identity. And when there is cultural conflict, questions of language always come to the fore. Tom Paulin, in his essay 'A New Look at the Language Question', reminds us that 'the history of a language is often a story of possession and dispossession, territorial struggle and the establishment or imposition of a culture' (178). Brian Friel, in a play such as *Translations*, demonstrates that what is lost in the act of translation can perhaps never be regained. Since cultural identity is laid into language it is not surprising that language can become the cause of a violent interaction between the colonized and the colonizer.

Seamus Deane, writing of Friel's play, cautions:

On the hither side of violence is Ireland as Paradise; on the nether side, Ireland as ruin. But, since we live on the nether side, we live in ruin and can only console ourselves with the desire for the paradise we briefly glimpse. The result is a discrepancy in our language; words are askew, they are out of line with fact. Violence has fantasy and wordiness as one of its most persistent after-effects. (171)

In their different ways, the artists reviewed in this paper recognise and interrogate these interrelationships of language, image, power, and violence. Michael Farrell moved from what he saw as the vacuity of an international abstract idiom for political engagement to a more literary, narrative style. In the early works of Willie Doherty and Paul Seawright, words are superimposed on images or accompanied by related and integral texts. Such composite works allow image and text to play off each other in order to extend meanings and readings, or in order for one to subvert the other. In Seawright's *Sectarian Murder* series, the cold text in each case acts as a key to unlock the tensions in the already contaminated locations where sectarian killings were carried out. On the other hand, in Willie Doherty's photoworks text is used in the most directly penetrative way. Floated over apparent photographic naturalism, they detonate meanings as if located within a shrapnel bomb. Rita Donagh, Michael Minnis, and Patrick Ireland all similarly deploy maps, networks, and text. Donagh graphically fixed the presence of the H-Blocks on the psychic landscape of Northern Ireland, while Minnis reminded us that maps are economical with truth, and Patrick Ireland used the grid (beloved by American Conceptual artists) as a pacing and sounding out platform for language. Philip Napier tests language for its wayward-ness, its purposeful ambiguities, opening up a range of uncertainties about the nature of an apology. In his monumental *Fragmens sur Les Institutions Républicaines*, Shane Cullen relates text to the body politic and to Republican idealism, and relates language to its location in myth and in the 'polis'.

As in other areas of conflict related to questions of cultural identity and the problematics of place, questions of language always seem to come to the fore. The artists discussed in this essay all recognise that culture, history, landscape, and memory are all layerings and that language is a process of writings, re-writings, overwritings, and underwritings – whatever you say, say nothing!

(Some parts of this text have been previously published in *Thinking Long – Contemporary Art in the North of Ireland*, Gandon Editions, Kinsale, 1996.)

WORKS CITED

Barrett, Cyril. *Michael Farrell.* Dublin: Douglas Hyde Gallery, 1979.
Cullen, Shane. *Fragmens sur les Institutions Republiciaines IV.* 1997. Panels 1–96. Orchard Gallery, Derry.
Deane, Seamus. 'Brian Friel: the Double Stage'. *Celtic Revivals: Essays in Modern Irish Literature.* London: Faber and Faber, 1985. 166–73.
Doherty, Willie. *The Only Good One is a Dead One.* 1993. Matt's Gallery, London. Double-screen video projection with sound, size variable.
—. *Policy. Commitment and Policy: Investment.* 1989. Belfast. 183 x 183cm.
—. *Same Difference.* 1990. Matt's Gallery, London. Audio/slide installation.
—. *Strategy. Sever and Strategy: Isolate.* 1989. Belfast, Westlink. Black and white photograph with text. 122 x 183cm.
—. *The Walls.* 1987. Black and white photograph with text. 61 x 152.5cm
Donagh, Rita. *Cellular Maze.* 1983. Exhibition at Orchard Gallery, Derry.
—. *Long Meadow.* 1982. Oil on canvas. 152 x 152cm.
—. *Shadow of Six Counties.* 1970–. Pencil and gouache on map. 36 x 36cm.

Ellmann, Maud. *The Hunger Artists: Starving, Writing and Imprisonment.* London: Virago, 1993.

Farrell, Michael. *Madonna Irlanda.* 1977. Painting.

—. *Pressé.* Series, 1970–.

—. *Pressé Politique.* 1973. Painting with one floor piece.

—. *Une autre nature morte a la mode Irlandaise.* 1975–76. Collage on wood. 100 x 100cm.

Fisher, Jean. *Willie Doherty, Unknown Depths.* Exhibition catalogue. Cardiff: Fotogallery, Derry: Orchard Gallery, and Glasgow: Third Eye Centre, 1990.

Gibbons, Luke. 'Space, Place and Public Art: Sligo and its Surroundings'. *Placing Art – a Colloquium on Public Art in Rural, Coastal, and Small Urban Environments.* Ed. L. Kelly. Sligo: Sligo County Council, 2002.

Ireland, Patrick. *BIG H.* 1989. Rope drawing installation. Orpheus Gallery, Belfast.

—. *Purgatory.* 1985. Mixed media installation. Douglas Hyde Gallery, Dublin.

Krauss, Rosalind. *The Originality of the Avante-Garde and Other Modernist Myths.* Cambridge, Mass. and London: MIT Press, 1986.

Minnis, Michael. *Street Index.* 1993. Oil on aluminium.

Moore, Brian. *Lies of Silence.* London: Bloomsbury Books, 1990.

McEvilley, Tom. *Philip Napier, Gauge.* Exhibition catalogue. Derry: Orchard Gallery, 1998.

Napier, Philip. *Gauge.* 1997. Installation. Orchard Gallery and Glenfada Park, Derry.

Paulin, Tom. 'A New Look at the Language Question'. *Ireland and the English Crisis.* Newcastle-upon-Tyne: Bloodaxe, 1984. 178–193.

Rogoff, Irit. 'The Case for Critical Cartographics'. *Cartographics: Geo-gnostic Projection for the 21st Century.* Ed. Zelimar Koscevic. Zagreb: Muzej Suvremene Umjetnosti, 1997. 144–149.

Seawright, Paul. *Sectarian Murders.* 1987–1988. Series of 15 photographs. C-type prints 101x101cm.

Wilson, Mike. *Shane Cullen: Fragmens sur les Institutions Republicaines IV.* Derry: Orchard Gallery / Limousin: Centre d'art contemporain de Vassiviere en Limousin, 1997.

Contributors

BRIAN CLIFF is a Brittain Fellow at the Georgia Institute of Technology (Atlanta). His research areas include modern and contemporary Irish literature. Selected publications: '"as assiduously advertised": Publicizing the 1899 Irish Literary Theatre Season', in *Critical Ireland: New Essays in Literature and Culture*, ed. Alan Gillis and Aaron Kelly (Four Courts Press, 2001). 'Crossing through the *Borderlands*', in *The Theatre of Frank McGuinness: Stages of Mutability*, ed. Helen Lojek (Carysfort Press, 2002). '"Whither thou goest": The Possibility of Community in *Observe the Sons of Ulster Marching Towards the Somme* and *Someone Who'll Watch over Me*', in *Foilsiú* 3.1 (Spring 2003). 'Paul Muldoon's Community "on the cusp": Auden and MacNeice in the Manuscripts for "7, Middagh Street"', in *Contemporary Literature* 44.4 (Winter 2003). He is currently at work on a book, *Border Writing: Community and Contemporary Irish Literature.*

ANNE DEVLIN is a playwright, short story writer, and a critic. Her stories include *The Way-Paver* (1986), and her plays include *Ourselves Alone* (1986) and *After Easter* (1994). She also wrote the film script for *Titanic Town* (1999).

DEREK HAND lectures in St Patrick's College, Drumcondra. His research areas include Irish writing, the novel, and literary theory. Selected publications: *John Banville: Exploring Fictions* (Liffey Press, 2002). 'Breaking Boundaries, Creating Spaces: W.B Yeats's *The Words upon the Window-Pane* as a Post-colonial Text', in *W.B. Yeats and Post-colonialism*, ed. Deborah Fleming (Locust Hill Press, 2001). 'Being Ordinary: Ireland from Elsewhere: A reading of Éilís Ní Dhuibhne's *The Bray House*', in *Irish University Review* 30.1 (Spring/Summer 2000). 'The Ontological Imperative in Irish Writing', in the *Brazilian Journal of Irish Studies* 5 (June 2003).

RICHARD HASLAM lectures in the Department of English at Saint Joseph's University in Philadelphia. His research areas include nineteenth- and twentieth-century Irish fiction in English, Irish film, and Irish literary and cultural theory. Selected publications: '"A race bashed in the face": Imagining Ireland as a Damaged Child', in *Jouvert: a journal of postcolonial studies* 4.1 (Fall 1999) <http://social.chass.ncsu.edu/jouvert>. '"Designed to cause suffering": *Cal* and the Politics of Imprisonment', in *Nua: Studies in Contemporary Irish Writing* III.1–2 (2002). 'Neil Jordan and the ABC of Narratology: "Stories to do with love are mathematical"', in *New Hibernia*

Review 3.2 (Summer 1999). "'The Pose Arranged and Lingered Over": Visualizing the "Troubles"', in *Contemporary Irish Fiction: Themes, Tropes, Theories*, ed. Liam Harte and Michael Parker (St Martin's Press, 2000).

CELIA KEENAN is lecturer in English and Director of the MA Programme in children's literature at St Patrick's College, Drumcondra, and President of the Irish Society for the Study of Children's Literature. Her research areas include children's literature, Irish children's literature, historical fiction for children, children's film, and visual culture. Selected publications: Co-editor, with Valerie Coghlan, *The Big Guide to Irish Children's Books* (Irish Children's Books Trust, 1996). Co-editor, with Valerie Coghlan, *The Big Guide 2: Irish Children's Books* (Irish Children's Books Trust, 2000). 'Narrative Challenges: The Great Irish Famine in Recent Stories for Children', in *The Presence of the Past in Children's Literature*, ed. Ann Lawson Lucas (Praeger, 2003).

LIAM KELLY is a Professor of Irish Visual Culture at the School of Art and Design, University of Ulster, Belfast. He is a writer and broadcaster on contemporary Irish art. He has also curated both solo and thematic exhibitions in Ireland, USA, France, Slovenia, and Hong Kong. He took part in *L'imaginaire Irlandais* as curator of *Language Mapping and Power*, exhibited in Paris in 1996. From 1986–1992 he was Director of the Orpheus Gallery in Belfast, and from 1996–1999 Director of the Orchard Gallery in Derry. Selected publications: *Thinking Long: Contemporary Art in the North of Ireland* (1996) and *The City as Art: Interrogating the Polis* (1994). He is currently a vice-president of the International Association of Art Critics, Paris (AICA). In 1997 he organized their international annual congress, *Art and Centres of Conflict – Outer and Inner Realities* in Belfast and Derry.

JOZEFINA KOMPORÁLY is a research associate at the University of Hull. Her research areas include literature, gender, and identity; twentieth century and contemporary British and Irish theatre; women's playwriting and feminist theatre; the history of European theatre; and literature and translation. Selected publications: 'De-sexing the Maternal: Reproductive Technologies and Male Medical Authority in Contemporary British Women's Drama', in *Gramma: Journal of Theory and Criticism* 10 (2002). "'Channels (France)": A Translation Exchange for French Plays into English', in *New Theatre Quarterly* 74 (May 2003). 'Motherhood, Female Lineage, Authorship: Rewriting British Women's Theatre', *B.A.S.: British and American Studies* IX (2003). "'Let me remember who I am": Maternal Love and Exile as Quests for Identity in Timberlake Wertenbaker's *Credible Witness*', in *Selves at Home, Selves in*

Exile: Stories of Emplacement and Displacement, proceedings of the Seventh Cultural Studies Symposium (Department of American and English Culture and Literature, Ege University, Izmir, Turkey, 2003).

GERARDINE MEANEY lectures in the Department of English at University College, Dublin. Her research areas include cultural theory, feminist theory, gender and culture in Ireland, and women's writing. Selected publications: *(Un)like Subjects: Women, Theory, Fiction* (Routledge, 1993). Co-editor *Field Day Anthology: Women's Writing and Traditions*, Volume 4 and 5 (Cork UP, 2002). *Nora* (Cork UP, 2004).

J'AIME MORRISON is Assistant Professor of Theatre and Dance at California State University, Northridge. Her research areas include dance, performance studies, and Irish Studies. Selected Publications: 'Irish choreo-cinema: Dancing at the Crossroads of Language and Performance', in *Yale Journal of Criticism* 15.1 (2002). 'Dancing between Decks: Choreographies of Transition during Irish Migrations to America', in *Eire/Ireland* 36 (2001). 'Talking Feet-Talking Cure', in *Film Ireland* 72 (August-September, 1999).

DES O'RAWE lectures in Film Studies at Queen's University, Belfast. His research areas include Irish visual and literary culture, and cinema aesthetics. Selected Publications: 'At Home with Horror: Neil Jordan's Gothic Variations', in *Irish Studies Review* 11.2 (2003). 'Beyond Representation: *I Could Read the Sky* and Irish Cinema', in *Canadian Journal of Irish Studies* (2003). Co-editor, with Eamonn Hughes and Edna Longley, *Ireland (Ulster) Scotland: Concepts, Contexts and Comparisons* (Queen's University Press, 2003). *The Shot* (Manchester UP, forthcoming 2004).

GLENN PATTERSON is a novelist and cultural commentator. His novels include *Burning Your Own* (1988), *Fat Lad* (1992), *The International* (1999), and *Number 5* (2002).

BILL ROLSTON is Professor of Sociology at University of Ulster, Jordanstown. His research areas include wall murals and political identity, and mass media. Selected Publications: 'Assembling the Jigsaw: Truth, Justice and Transition in the North of Ireland,' in *Race and Class* 44.1 (2002). *Drawing Support 3: Murals and Transition in the North of Ireland* (Beyond the Pale Publications, 2003). 'Bring it All Back Home: Irish Emigration and Racism', in *Race and Class* 45.2 (2003).

JAYNE STEEL lectures in English and Creative Writing at Lancaster University. Drawing upon Lacanian psychoanalysis and cultural materialism, her research areas include representations of the political conflict in the north of Ireland in fiction, film, and the media. Her academic work has been published in England (*Irish Studies Review*), Ireland *(Irish Review)*, and North America (*Journal of Psychoanalysis, Culture, and Society*). She has a forthcoming chapter in *Soldiers, New Women and Wicked Hags* (Irish Academic Press*)*. In addition to her academic work, Jayne is an award-winning screenwriter.

COLM TÓIBÍN is a novelist, critic, and travel writer. His novels include *The South* (1990), *The Heather Blazing* (1993), and *The Blackwater Lightship* (1999). He has also written *Homage to Barcelona* (1989) and *Travels in Catholic Europe* (1994).

ÉIBHEAR WALSHE lectures in English at University College, Cork. His research areas include modern Irish drama, Munster women writers, and Irish lesbian and gay writing. Selected Publications: *Ordinary People Dancing: Essays on Kate O'Brien* (Cork UP, 1993). *Sex, Nation, and Dissent* (Cork UP, 1997). *Elizabeth Bowen Remembered* (Four Courts Press, 1999). *The Plays of Teresa Deevy* (Mellen Press, 2003).

Index